Under the
Shade Tree

Seeking & Trusting God through Worship

GAIL GRAHAM

Cover Art by Heather Ragsdale
Cover and Interior Layout @ 2024 Harvest Creek Publishing and Design

www.harvestcreek.net email: info@harvestcreek.net

Ordering Information: Special discounts are available on quantity purchases by groups, churches, and other associations.

For details, please contact the author using the information provided at the back of this book.

Under the Shade Tree—1st edition.

ISBN: 978-1-961641-18-1

Printed in the United States of America

Table of Contents

Dedication

Humbly I dedicate *Under the Shade Tree* to Almighty God, who is my Creator, my Salvation through the sacrificial blood of Jesus Christ, and my Abundant Life through the power of the Holy Spirit. My heart continuously praises God for His faithfulness in my life as I learn to trust Him and depend on Him instead of living in self-pity during the struggles of life on this earth. What gratitude I have for the steadfast love that God gives His people as they honor Him in their worship times while experiencing the realities of life. What a blessing to know God and to worship in His presence! Glory be to God for the joy and the peace that only He can give us.

It is with much love and my precious memories that I also dedicate what God has given me in my times *under the shade trees* to my beloved husband, Max. Our fifty-year marriage was filled with blessings, love for our Lord, and daily love and respect for each other as we faithfully upheld our wedding vows. It is with a grateful heart that I honor my husband for his deep love, enduring patience, kind-hearted actions, and faithfulness to me as we held hands in loving and serving our Lord together.

Acknowledgments

To my late husband, Max, who lovingly shared my walk with God and supported me in my love of writing.

Dr. Jeff Berger, you constantly motivate your congregation to seek God's guidance in their relationships with others. You are my pastor and my friend, who has a listening ear and a caring heart. Thank you for supporting me throughout my experiences *under the shade trees*.

To my friend, Heather Ragsdale, thank you for your beautiful watercolor painting for the cover of this book. Throughout my writing and my time of shade tree experiences, you have loved and supported me with encouragement and prayer. I thank God for your sweet spirit and artistic talents.

To Dr. Jeff Berger, Carol Homan, Dr. Pat Nichol, Heather Ragsdale, and Stephanie Chatfield for editing this manuscript and encouraging me to publish it and share it with the women in our congregation at First Baptist Church, Conroe. I am grateful for your loving prayers. What a blessing to witness over fifty women gather every Monday morning for nine weeks to study *Under the Shade Tree!* It was such a sweet time reading and discussing scriptures, joining in prayer, and singing hymns. Thanks to our media pastor, Jaymes Brown, for helping provide videos of the hymns with lyrics each week.

To Ryann Bayer and Abbie Ripple for your love and support. Witnessing the involvement of our MOPS group (**M**others **of** **P**reschoolers) was a true blessing. These young mothers could share and read scriptures on topics like Seeking God, Loving Family and Friends, and Trusting God in the Realities of Life. I pray their involvement will have a lasting impact on their spiritual growth.

Preface

These pages record the blessings that God revealed to me during my time of worship *under the shade tree* from 2020 to 2021. I experienced God in the realities of life with the COVID threat in our world and through illness, death, and grief in my family. God was visible in every aspect of life throughout those days, and I learned so much more about His faithfulness.

Prayers, scriptures, and hymns have helped me express what God gave me through those times of my life. I hope these pages bless you and allow you to express your thoughts and experiences as you read them. You can expect a deeper understanding of God's Holy Word and a worshipful experience with anointed hymns.

I thank God for my times *under the shade trees* as I continue to praise Him daily for His goodness and loving care, which brings me much peace and joy in my life.

As you learn about God in my life, I hope you'll also encounter Him on your own and share your story of His faithfulness.

Gail Graham

Foreword

I met Gail Graham for the first time over eight years ago. Gail and two other people—all strangers to me then but who would become my dear friends—showed up at my church in Houston on a Sunday morning. Their church in Conroe was looking for a pastor, and they were there to see if I was worth considering. They were part of what (in Baptist life) is called a "Pastor Search Team."

That day marked the beginning of an emotional experience for my wife and me. After six months of prayer and many conversations with the Team, we left a wonderful church to become Gail's pastor and friend. Right from the start, she and her husband, Max, proved themselves to be the real deal.

Max, a former college athlete turned coach, was now a gentle, faithful example of Christlike masculinity. He was a man I wished I could replicate a thousand times over. Gail was a retired teacher whose Jesus-serving engine had no "off" button! She taught ESL classes, sang in the choir, and led our women's ministry with tireless passion. She always seemed to have new ideas for ways to do more for the Lord.

During the pandemic, Max's battle with cancer reached a critical stage. Like so many other families during that awful time, he and Gail had to navigate uncharted territory, including well-intentioned regulations that separated a husband and wife when they needed each other the most. Gail, stuck outside a hospital during a blistering Texas summer to boot and worried about the man she loved, had no one to turn to but Jesus.

When Max passed away, her closeness to Christ only deepened as she grieved. Gail had been in church her whole life. She knew Romans 8:28 by heart. For countless times, she had sung "Great is Thy Faithfulness," a hymn based on Jeremiah's words in the aftermath of devastation. And she had heard repeatedly how God could bring beauty from ashes. But now, she experienced it firsthand. This book was born amidst tears, loneliness, grief, and the first lessons of living alone.

When she finished writing, she asked me if it was appropriate for her to use this as a curriculum for our ladies' Bible study group. After reading her words, I had no doubt. Everyone I know is fighting a battle of some kind, though few let the rest of us know about it. They needed to know it was okay to struggle and that it was alright to ask God the difficult questions.

Most of all, they needed to know that when they cried out, there was someone there to hear—One who Himself had suffered grief. After all, the God of Scripture is not like man-made gods: He knows what it's like to grieve the loss of an only Son. He keeps our tears in a bottle. And He will redeem every one of them if we trust Him in the dark.

Whatever battle you are fighting, I know this book will help. The One who was with Gail *under the shade tree* outside that hospital is the Savior who bore your sorrows at the cross. May He bless you as He blessed her with a new understanding of just how wonderful He is. May you find, as Gail did, that He is more than enough.

Dr. Jeff Berger
Sr. Pastor, 1st Baptist Church, Conroe, TX

Introduction

During the COVID-19 time in the spring of 2020, I found myself parked in my car *under a shade tree* at the Houston Methodist Medical Center in The Woodlands, Texas. No one could accompany patients during that time. These shade tree occasions became almost a weekly routine because of my husband's appointments.

The first time *under the shade tree* was on Friday, March 27, for seven hours while my husband underwent a surgical procedure at the hospital. I carried a bag with me that contained my Bible, books, writing supplies, and snacks. Yes, my eyes teared up as my husband, Max, parked the car *under a shade tree* in front of the hospital. He gave me a goodbye kiss as he always did, and I kept my eyes on him until he entered the door of the hospital. He looked so alone, and I felt alone while watching him, as I did not know what the day would be like.

Soon, I discovered texts on my phone that continued all day from my children, my husband's sister, my sisters, and friends, as well as many of my adult English Second Language students. Throughout the day, I received phone calls from my family and close friends. Some prayed with me on the phone. What an encouragement that was!

It was a reminder that God uses His people to show His love and care. Even though I was the only person in the car at that time, I was definitely not alone. On that day, I experienced an extraordinary and overwhelming encounter with the Spirit of God.

It took us close to an hour to drive home from the hospital after my husband was released. That was the beginning of our many long months of staying at home. We found ourselves "shut in" because of the pandemic. With his low blood counts, we avoided all possibilities of contracting the virus.

Sitting *under the shade trees* at the medical center for months, I came to appreciate the multitude of ways God blessed my time there. For example:

- ✓ The trees were a welcome sight in this massive area of concrete.
- ✓ The landscapers strategically planted them to provide shade for the parking lot.
- ✓ The trees' strong roots provided them with support and growth, reminding me of my roots and the loving support that nurtured my Christian faith.

On those days, I found pleasure in the breeze that flowed through the trees while my windows were down. Supporting my husband for fifty years brought me a sense of safety and security. Most times, I would be the one driving us back home.

During the first few weeks, my heart felt a tug to write about God and the realities of life with scriptures. I had just put it aside, but God's calling seemed so strong. So, I listened to his voice concerning my writing.

One day, while sitting *under the shade tree*, I enjoyed a phone visit with my friend Mary Margaret, and the Spirit just led me to ask her for prayer support. She immediately began weeping, voiced a prayer, and expressed her excitement that I was following God in such an endeavor. I thank God for her sweet friendship and her daily lifting me up to the Father.

Each day during the pandemic, my husband and I set aside an hour for personal time with God. He would go to our bedroom to read his Bible while listening to Christian radio. The living room then became my place to worship while playing the piano and singing hymns. During that time, God led me to scriptures and songs to include in my writings. I felt thankful for this opportunity to really focus on God's plan, which included singing hymns and praises to Him.

Worship through Bible study, prayer, and music has always been a vital part of my relationship with God. Being a lifelong churchgoer and becoming a Christian as a child has brought me closer to God. His love and guidance have been consistent through the years. Taking part in many Bible studies has given me a sound knowledge of God's Word.

However, during the pandemic, my heart yearned for more. I desired a more substantial daily worship time with a more profound sense of His presence in my life. It didn't take long to discover that this desire would reveal God to me in ways never experienced before.

Throughout those days, I wanted to know more about God: the Father, the Son, and the Holy Spirit. Acknowledgment of the Trinity has always been especially important in my life. During that time, I developed a greater desire to seek God and to see Him in all circumstances.

So, spending more time with God in His Word with the guidance of the Holy Spirit became a highlight of each day. It was a way to truly know and encounter more of God, especially in the reality of the tough days of life.

Much of my time of worship and seeking God was *under the shade trees* at the medical center or in our backyard. The more time I spent there, the stronger my conviction grew that God had intended it to be a place where I could experience His presence even more deeply. I believe God wanted me to experience His loving care in those realities of life and to hear His voice while sitting *under the shade trees.*

> Then the LORD will create over all of Mount Zion and over those who assemble there a cloud of smoke by day and a glow of flaming fire by night; over everything the glory will be a canopy. It will be a shelter and shade from the heat by day, and a refuge and hiding place from the storm and the rain.
>
> ISAIAH 4:5 NIV

This scripture reminds me of God's provision and loving care, especially on days *under the shade tree* and during the daily struggles of life. These pages express worship each day, along with experiences of illness, fears, grief, loneliness, and much more. The blessings are to experience God's unwavering love and care in the realities of life.

In my sanctuary, God's love surrounds me as I find joy, peace, and songs of praise, trusting in God Almighty. Resting in His care is the best place to know Him and listen to Him genuinely. Despite our awareness of God's presence everywhere, I long for everyone to find a unique place to worship and connect with Him. This will be a place where we can experience all He has for each of us as we continue life on Earth.

> Whoever dwells in the shelter of the Most High will rest in the shadow of the Almighty. I will say of the LORD, "He is my refuge and my fortress, my God, in whom I trust"
>
> PSALM 91:1-2 NIV

> ...speaking to one another with psalms, hymns, and spiritual songs from the Spirit. Sing and make music in your heart to the Lord, always giving thanks to God the Father for everything, in the name of our Lord Jesus Christ.
>
> EPHESIANS 5:19-20 NIV

KNOWING GOD IN UNEXPECTED CHALLENGES

O God, I am so grateful for Your loving care of us when unexpected events suddenly seem to overcome our lives.

In February 2020, after learning that the coronavirus was in China, I texted my friend and ESL student to determine if she was in Texas or China. She lives in the United States but often goes to China to see her mother, especially during the Chinese New Year celebrations.

I learned she was in Texas. She was concerned about her family in China and had even mailed masks to them. On Sunday morning, I asked my Life Group to pray for her, her family, and those in China. We did not know that the virus would soon have a profound impact on the entire world, including us in Texas.

The first week of March was busy. I taught English as a Second Language lesson at church two mornings a week and hosted lunch with my students at a local restaurant. That week, I accompanied my husband to two doctor's appointments. During the third week of March, while attending a committee meeting at the church, I was told that our church would be closed until further notice.

There would be no gatherings at the church because of the county government restrictions to keep people safe from the virus. I immediately contacted ladies who attended our Monday Morning Bible study and our ESL students to inform them of the cancelations. I remembered how my husband and I had served as greeters at the main doors to the sanctuary the previous Sunday. We had shaken a few hands and used hand sanitizer often because of the rumors of the virus.

Life as my husband, Max, and I knew it immediately changed: no more ESL classes, no more driver's education classes for him, not being in the church building, and no going shopping. The only place my husband and I could go was to medical appointments, which eventually turned into telephone conferences with doctors. By the end of March, only patients could go into medical buildings with screening at the entrances, and masks were required.

Even as we experienced these unexpected events, I sensed in my heart that our all-knowing, loving God would be with us and take care of us.

YOUR THOUGHTS

✓ What is your recollection of the start of the pandemic?
✓ How did you observe God supporting you during the sudden transition?

_____

_____

_____

_____

_____

_____

_____

_____

_____

_____

_____

GOD'S WORD

❖ *The eyes of the LORD are everywhere, keeping watch on the evil and the good.*
Proverbs 15:3

❖ *But the eyes of the LORD are on those who fear him, on those whose hope is in his unfailing love, to deliver them from death and keep them alive in famine.* Psalm 33:18-19

❖ *But he who unites himself with the Lord is one with him in Spirit.* Philippians 4:19

HYMN FOR TODAY:

 God Will Take Care of You (Civilla D. Martin, Author, 1904)

> *God, I thank You that we can depend on*
> *Your guidance as we enter this surreal time.*

Sitting on our deck *under the shade tree* one morning, I realized that the upcoming days could be challenging. So, I prayed for God to guide us in His care. My husband and I were trying to keep up with all the news of the virus in our country and around the world. We realized we needed to prepare for the weeks ahead.

So, I did an inventory of my kitchen, made menus, and cooked three meals a day, and I enjoyed doing so. Preparing our meals was easy, but being totally isolated from other people was not so easy. With the realization of how the virus spread so rapidly and my husband's blood disease, we immediately knew that we needed to stay in our house.

Our only social contacts were with cards in the mail, phone calls, texts, and emails. These soon became important because the social media posts and messages helped with encouraging words. Yet, most vital for Max and me was continuing to communicate daily with God through His Word, prayers, and watching Bible teaching on television. Early mornings on the deck, listening to the birds sing in the quiet of the mornings, became one of my favorite times of the day.

The more we watched the television news reports, the more unreal this all seemed. A worldwide pandemic has taken so many lives and totally changed the way people live. Words such as coronavirus, COVID-19, quarantine, government daily briefings, masks, gloves, social distancing, and stay-at-home orders have taken over our lives. The only places to shop were for essential needs, and many of those places had empty shelves, and people had to stand in long lines six feet apart to go in a few at a time.

Yes, it all was surreal, and our society had to learn how to live in such a fast-changing world. It was a time to know God truly and to seek His guidance. Max and I felt blessed to know that we would find our stronghold in God for refuge and strength.

YOUR THOUGHTS

✓ What did you see as your most critical need in preparing for the pandemic?
✓ Were you prepared for your social and spiritual needs?

_____

_____

_____

_____

_____

_____

_____

_____

_____

_____

GOD'S WORD

❖ _I will instruct you and teach you in the way you should go; I will counsel you and watch over you._ Psalm 32:8

❖ _In their hearts, humans plan their course, but the LORD establishes their steps._ Proverbs 16:9

❖ _The Lord is a refuge for the oppressed, a stronghold in times of trouble. Those who know your name trust in you, for you, LORD, have never forsaken those who seek you._ Psalm 9:9-10

❖ _God is our refuge and strength, an ever-present help in trouble._ Psalm 46:1

HYMN FOR TODAY:

 A Mighty Fortress Is Our God (Martin Luther, Author, 1529 and Frederic H. Hedge, Translator, 1852)

God, how do I know You? How can I trust in You when I cannot see You?

As a young child, my parents and teachers at church taught me that God is love, and that *Jesus loves me*. Even without seeing God, I've always held onto the conviction of His existence. Growing up in the church and enjoying reading the Bible for myself, I learned so much more about God.

Sitting *under the shade tree* one day at the hospital, I began again to ponder about the God that I had always trusted. Who is He? Why do I trust Him? Where do I find my answers? Of course, I went to God's Word again to search for more. Seeing God in the lives of the Bible characters reminds me that God is *Spirit*, and God is *Holy*, and He is *Powerful*. That is how I sit *under a shade tree* and worship Him through the sanctity of the Holy Spirit. I know I can trust that Spirit as I sense His presence. I can see the evidence of God in His creation and His care for those who genuinely trust in Him.

Throughout the Bible, we can see God's power in dealing with people and nature, as well as the miraculous birth and resurrection of Jesus. Yes, it is through the power of Jesus's sacrificial blood that I am a believer and can come to the Father and trust in Him. I can see His Spirit living in people. And sometimes, we fail to acknowledge how powerful our God truly is. But the God that I worship is living and breathing in me.

God created me, and He understands my struggles in life here on earth. His power provides all my needs as I trust Him to do so. Yes, the power of God is real and active in my life, and even as Satan tells me to doubt, I must always trust God with faith. I pray for all to know the one true God. All glory and honor be to God!

YOUR THOUGHTS

- ✓ What questions do you have about God, and have you found answers to them?
- ✓ How do you explain knowing God and trusting Him?

_____

_____

_____

_____

_____

_____

_____

_____

_____

_____

GOD'S WORD

- ❖ *Now the earth was formless and empty, darkness was over the surface of the deep, and the Spirit of God was hovering over the waters.* Genesis 1:2

- ❖ *The Spirit of God has made me; the breath of the Almighty gives me life.* Job 33:4

- ❖ *He determines the number of the stars and calls them each by name. Great is our Lord, and mighty in power; His understanding has no limit.* Psalm 147:4-5

- ❖ *Yet for us there is but one God, the Father, from whom all things came and for whom we live; and there is but one Lord, Jesus Christ, through whom all things came and through whom we live.* I Corinthians 8:6

❖ *For since the creation of the world God's invisible qualities—his eternal power and divine nature—have been clearly seen, being understood from what has been made, so that people are without excuse.* Romans 1:20

❖ *Now to the King eternal, immortal, invisible, the only God, be honor and glory for ever and ever. Amen.* I Timothy 1:17

HYMN FOR TODAY:

 Immortal, Invisible, God Only Wise (Walter C. Smith, 1867)

Lord, I praise Your name as I join the chorus.
What a beautiful rendition of sounds for You,
our Almighty God!

Early one morning, as I sat on the deck *under the shade tree* for my worship time, the birds seemed to be making "a joyful noise" with so many different sounds. It reminded me of people around the world singing praises to God in their different languages. I think amidst the praises, some of God's people were crying out to Him for help and healing.

It was interesting to observe that as the chorus of birds grew from a few too many, it became louder. I think God must be so pleased with this and to believe that those choruses of the birds are happening all around the world. The thought came to me that the louder people voice their praises with their faithful acknowledgment of God, the more people will hear and join in the chorus. The world needs to hear Christians praising our Holy God! It is such a beautiful way to share Him with others!

Praising God in the power of the Holy Spirit helps us to acknowledge who He is in our lives. Praising Him daily keeps us in a strong relationship with God as we experience His faithfulness to us. My prayer is for many more people to join this Praise Team. It is so awesome to worship God with all His creation and that He can speak to us in the simple beauty of the birds singing.

YOUR THOUGHTS

✓ Tell about some of your worship experiences while listening to God's creation.
✓ How can praising God be a testimony of your faith in God?

_____

_____

_____

_____

_____

_____

_____

_____

_____

GOD'S WORD

❖ *All the earth bows down to you; they sing praise to you. They sing the praises of your name.* Psalm 66:4

❖ *Praise the LORD. Praise God in his sanctuary; praise him in his mighty heavens.* Psalm 150:1

❖ *Let everything that has breath praise the LORD. Praise the LORD.* Psalm 150:6

❖ *All the nations you have made will come and worship before you, LORD; they will bring glory to your name. For you are great and do marvelous deeds; you alone are God.* Psalm 86:9-10

❖ *Sing to the LORD, for he has done glorious things; let this be made known to all the world.* Isaiah 12:5

HYMN FOR TODAY:

 All People that on Earth Do Dwell/Doxology (William Kethe, 1650)

Holy, Holy, Holy (Lyrics by Reginald Heber, Melody by John B. Dykes, 1861)

> *You, O God, are worthy of our praise as we see Your majesty in all creation.*

During one of my first times *under the shade tree* at the hospital, I focused my thoughts on "What does God want from His creation?" I remembered the times over the years when my husband and I were privileged to spend time in the Rocky Mountains. What a joy for our family to participate in huddle groups with students and adults from all over the USA at Fellowship of Christian Athletes camps! Those were such special times, sitting *under shade trees* studying God's Word, sharing words of testimony, and praying with others.

I will always treasure the times that Max and I spent at The Glen Eyrie Castle and Conference Center in Colorado Springs. My heart is filled with gratitude for the last time that Max and I were in the mountains. We were with friends for a church retreat in October 2019. We enjoyed the beauty of the Glen Eyrie Rose Garden while participating in the Lord's Supper and the gorgeous snowfall the next day.

Yes, the majesty and the beauty of the mountains remind me of the power of our awesome God, who created all that we enjoy. He is so worthy of our daily praise. We often find ourselves in awe of the grandeur of the mountains, and we tend to worship the *created* instead of the *Creator*. We are blessed to know God, the Creator, who desires that we have fellowship with Him. Yes, as we praise and worship God in His Holiness, we are so blessed with a sacred time that fulfills our spiritual needs, especially in our days of strife and struggles of life here on earth.

YOUR THOUGHTS

✓ How do you see God in His creation?

✓ Is worshiping God out in the beauty of His creation different from worshiping in a church building?

_____

_____

_____

_____

_____

_____

_____

_____

_____

GOD'S WORD

❖ *O, LORD, our Lord, how majestic your name is all over the earth! You have set Your glory above the heavens.* Psalm 8:1

❖ *When you look up into the sky and see the sun, the moon, and the stars—all the heavenly array—do not be enticed into bowing down to them and worshiping things the Lord your God has apportioned to all the nations under heaven.* Deuteronomy 4:19

❖ *In the beginning, God created the heavens and the earth. The earth was without form and an empty waste, and darkness was upon the face of the very great deep. The Spirit of God was moving over the face of the waters. And God said, "Let there be light and there was light."* Genesis 1:1-3

❖ *By the word of the LORD were the heavens made, their starry host by the breath of his mouth. He gathers the waters of the sea into jars; He puts the deep into storehouses. Let all the earth fear the LORD; let the people of the world revere him. For He spoke, and it came to be. He commanded, and it stood firm.*
Psalm 33:6-9

❖ *God brought me [wisdom] forth as the first of His works, before His deeds of old; I was appointed from eternity from the beginning before the world began.*
Proverbs 8:22-23

HYMN FOR TODAY:

Worthy of Worship (Dr. Terry York, 1988)
Glorify Thy Name (Donna Adkins, 1976)

> *Hear my cry, O Lord. Our country needs Your help in these days of confusion and uncertainty.*

I found myself *under the shade tree* for many days, either on my deck or at the hospital, and life seemed to become more unreal. My husband and I became part of a world with stay-at-home orders, wearing masks, and closed businesses. People were desperately distraught with this "monster" that had changed our lives. Not only were people ill or separated from society, but many were suffering because they could not be with their families. Our entire society seemed frustrated with what was happening in our country and upset that there appeared to be no answers.

People were crying out! Most of the crying out was to the government, complaining about the whole situation largely because our life of luxury and freedom had seemed to vanish. Perhaps some of this grumbling and protesting just demonstrated the selfish desires of the people. Yes, we needed answers and help with this virus that had invaded our world. I believed we needed to see more people "crying out to God" during this time. Yes, some were calling on God, but many were not.

People who know the one true Holy God will always go to Him because they know His grace and His faithfulness.

YOUR THOUGHTS

✓ What were some complaints made by the public?

✓ How would "crying out to God" make a difference?

✓ How do you think God answered those who were crying out to Him?

_____

_____

_____

_____

_____

_____

_____

_____

_____

GOD'S WORD

❖ *So the people grumbled against Moses, saying, "What are we to drink?" Then Moses cried out to the LORD, and the LORD showed him a piece of wood. He threw it into the water, and the water became fit to drink.* Exodus 15:24-25

❖ *The eyes of the LORD are on the righteous, and his ears are attentive to their cry. The righteous cry out, and the LORD hears them; he delivers them from all their troubles.* Psalm 34:15,17

❖ *Then they cried out to the LORD in their trouble, and he delivered them from their distress.* Psalm 107:6

❖ *The LORD is near to all who call on him, to all who call on him in truth.*
Psalm 145:18

❖ *Jesus said, "If you remain in me and my words remain in you, ask whatever you wish, and it will be done for you."* John 15:7

HYMN FOR TODAY:

Hear Our Prayer, O LORD (Anonymous)
God of Grace and God of Glory (Harry E. Fosdick, 1930)

> *God, today I pray for strangers. You know their hearts. I pray for their spiritual, physical, and emotional needs.*

Weeks went by and I continued to sit *under the shade tree* at Houston Methodist in The Woodlands, waiting for my husband as he went for blood tests and blood transfusions. There weren't many cars in the parking lots because only a few patients were coming for appointments. Since the virus had become so rampant in our state, there were many safety restrictions in place. Only patients were allowed to enter the medical facilities, and restrictions were placed on patients wearing masks and having their temperature taken as they entered the buildings. I saw many pregnant women going to appointments with a variety of masks on their faces. These were necessary appointments as they would soon give birth during this time.

One day, it was interesting to observe a young couple who parked next to me, put on their masks and gloves, then took their baby out of the car and completely covered him. The man took the baby to the hospital, and the lady went into the medical office building next to the hospital. I just began praying for them and their baby for God to protect them. Sometimes, I would see another person sitting in a car waiting. I would pray for them as well as the one on whom they were waiting. I prayed that they had a relationship with God and knew God's peace and healing. Yes, it was strange how wearing masks and waiting in parking lots had become our way of life. And that the Holy Spirit in my life inspired me to pray for people who were total strangers. Praying for them was important because I know God loves and cares for them. What a blessing to have a sweet closeness with the Father as I continued to pray for strangers while sitting in my car *under the shade tree.*

YOUR THOUGHTS

✓ Do you have a story about being at a medical facility during the pandemic?

✓ Recall times when you found yourself praying for strangers.

_____

_____

_____

_____

_____

_____

_____

_____

_____

_____

GOD'S WORD

❖ *And pray in the Spirit on all occasions with all kinds of prayers and requests. With this in mind, be alert and always keep praying for all the Lord's people.* Ephesians 6:18

❖ *In the same way, the Spirit helps us in our weakness. We do not know what we ought to pray for, but the Spirit himself intercedes for us.* Romans 8:26

❖ *Be joyful in hope, patient in affliction, faithful in prayer.* Romans 12:12

HYMN FOR TODAY

 Sweet Hour of Prayer (W. W. Walford, 1845)

> *Almighty God, help me have faith in the fears that tend to diminish the comfort and joy of the shade tree.*

On another day, while sitting on our deck *under the shade tree,* my memory took me back in time to one of the first shade tree experiences of my life. As a child, every summer, my siblings and I spent a week at our grandmother's house. My Granny lived in the deep woods in East Texas, where she had a sizeable garden, fruit trees, and chickens. She had a big shade tree with a swing on a rope in the front yard. My siblings, cousins, and I would take turns swinging in it. I liked it when it was my turn to swing.

The other children all learned that I was afraid of the chickens, so they would chase the chickens to me while I was in the swing to make me jump out and run away so one of them could grab the swing. Yes, I was so afraid of those chickens that I lost my joy of the swing. Living in fear can interfere with our enjoyment of the peace and comfort of the "shade" that God provides us.

During the COVID pandemic, there were so many things happening in the world to cause people to have worries or anxieties. In the beginning, because of little knowledge of the virus, news reports about how it spread appeared scary and confusing. Who really knew? Then, with a stay-at-home order, people became even more fearful. The news media informed us daily of the increasing number of COVID cases in our county and state, so we saw how it had affected all areas of our society. People needed to be cautious but not allow "anxiety" to control their lives. Staying in God's Word helped my husband and me to have faith over any fears during those months. God tells us to "not fear" but to trust in Him.

So, our faith in a loving God continued to give us joy, peace, and wisdom on how to live during those difficult times. Yes, I believe that our faith in God was a strong power that helped to raise us over any worries or fears that might control our lives.

YOUR THOUGHTS

✓ What are some fears people experience today?
✓ Name ways God has helped you through fearful times.

_____

_____

_____

_____

_____

_____

_____

_____

_____

_____

GOD'S WORD

❖ *It is the LORD who goes before you and will be with you; he will not leave you nor forsake you. Do not be afraid; do not be discouraged.* Deuteronomy 31:8

❖ *The Lord is my light and my salvation; whom shall I fear? The LORD is the stronghold of my life—of whom shall I be afraid?* Psalm 27:1

❖ *My soul finds rest in God alone; my salvation comes from him. He alone is my rock and my salvation; he is my fortress, and I will not be shaken.* Psalm 62:1-2

❖ *He will cover you with His feathers, and under his wings, you will find refuge; his faithfulness will be your shield and rampart. You will not fear the terror of the night, nor the arrow that flies by day, nor the pestilence that stalks in the darkness, not the plague that destroys at midday.* Psalm 91:4-5

HYMNS FOR TODAY

O Master, Let Me Walk with Thee (Washington Gladden)

You Raise Me Up (Josh Groban)

Dear God, help me to bring honor to You. I pray to never hide or cover Your Spirit in my life.

During the crazy time of the virus, people wore a variety of masks of various patterns and colors. During the pandemic, it became almost essential to wear a mask to cover our nose and mouth for protection. Most of us will agree that wearing those masks for long periods or just for a bit of a while really becomes annoying. I realized that in the reality of life, people sometimes wear masks to cover their true selves. Some people want to mask or cover up who they really are for fear of not being accepted or fitting in with a social group.

A few years ago. I saw a beautician who, in our many conversations, seemed to portray a Bible-reading Christian lady, and then one day, I saw her put on several masks with other customers. Her language with other customers was not the same as her conversation with me. Not to judge her, but who was she really? Perhaps all those other masks were just to fit in with the lifestyle of the person she was serving. If she had let God shine through, what a difference it might make in the lives of her customers.

Christians often are unaware that we sometimes wear a mask that hides who we are in Christ. We allow masks with the labels of "jealousy," "self-pity," and "insecurities" to hide our ability to show love and respect to others. Some wear a self-centered mask, which does no good. Of course, there is the mask of hypocrisy, which brings no honor to God. Sometimes, people wear a "church" mask and are busy just doing what they think they should do and boasting proudly about themselves, with no acknowledgment of God at all. Wearing masks can be a distraction and a hindrance to sharing God's truth.

Yes, there was always discussion of wanting to get rid of the mask mandate during the pandemic. But even today, let us, as Christians, get rid of all "masks" that hide who God is in our lives. Perhaps we need to think about the masks we wear and the messages those masks send to people who are seeking to see God in our lives. My prayer is that Christians live humbly consecrated lives so that our living God is glorified in us as a witness to others.

YOUR THOUGHTS

✓ How and why do we mask our true identities?
✓ Do we allow others to see God in us? Or do we cover it up with a "church" mask?
✓ How do we make sure we are honest with our identity as a Christian?

_____

_____

_____

_____

_____

_____

_____

_____

_____

GOD'S WORD

❖ *Nothing in all creation is hidden from God's sight. Everything is uncovered and laid bare before the eyes of him to whom we must give an account.* Hebrews 4:13

❖ *Jesus said, "When you give to the needy, do not let your left hand know what your right hand is doing, so that your giving may be in secret."* Matthew 6:3

❖ *Jesus said, "These people honor me with their lips, but their hearts are far from me. They worship me in vain; their teachings are merely human rules. You have let go of the commands of God and are holding on to the traditions of man."* Mark 7:6-8

❖ *Those who look to him are radiant; their faces are never covered with shame.* Psalm 34:5

❖ *We pray this so that the name of our Lord Jesus may be glorified in you, and you in him, according to the grace of our God and Lord Jesus Christ.* 2 Thessalonians 1:12

HYMNS FOR TODAY

Lord, Be Glorified (Bob Kilpatrick,1978)
Take My Life, and Let It Be Consecrated (Frances R. Havergal)

SEEKING GOD IN DAILY STRUGGLES

My husband and I were enjoying our time together, but we both missed being with other people. God wants people to share in His love, grace, and goodness. He so desires that we love people. The loneliness of those days seemed to be, indeed, a time when everyone needed to experience God's love.

Feeling so isolated and not being able to serve with others physically, I sought God's guidance in ways to share His love. I was missing my adult English Second Language students and was concerned about their safety and health. I wrote a letter to each student and sent them a self-addressed, stamped envelope so they could write a letter to me.

In the previous January, our Care Givers Life Group had adopted the Esther Sunday morning Bible study class at church. So it seemed important to write a personal note to each of those ladies who are in their late eighties or nineties. Calling friends who live alone was a pleasure. Sending encouraging notes to friends in our church was another way to minister to people. It was good for Max to walk outside and social distance while visiting with a guy in the neighborhood. It surely brightened up his day.

All the while, we received many texts, cards, letters, and emails from friends and some family members who lovingly ministered to us. What encouragement for us! We knew that all this sharing was done only in the power of the love of our God, who was lifting us up to Him during such a time of missing Christian fellowship in person. Yes, sharing God's love as Jesus has commanded us to do will always shine brightly in our days and glorify our Father in heaven.

YOUR THOUGHTS

✓ What are some ways you allowed God to use you to reach out to others?

✓ In what ways did others show God's love to you when you were in need?

_____

_____

_____

_____

_____

_____

_____

_____

_____

_____

GOD'S WORD

❖ *Do everything in love.* I Corinthians 16:14

❖ *Dear friends, since God so loved us, we also ought to love one another. No one has seen God, but if we love one another, God lives in us, and his love is made complete in us.* I John 4:11-12

❖ *And the King will reply, "Truly, I tell you, whatever you did for one of the least of these brothers and sisters of mine, you did for me."* Matthew 25:40

❖ *No one should seek their own good, but the good of others.* I Corinthians 10:24

❖ *Serve wholeheartedly as if you were serving the Lord, not people.* Ephesians 6:7

❖ *Jesus said, "Let your light so shine before men, that they may see your good deeds and praise your Father in heaven."* Matthew 5:16

HYMN FOR TODAY

 Shine, Jesus, Shine (Graham Kendrick,1988)

Dear Heavenly Father, my heart is seeking
more of Your holiness and power.

When I wake up each day, I lie in bed and pray to my Heavenly Father; this has been my practice for many years. He has given me much encouragement and help during those times of communication with Him. He is my "Father," and I desire to seek Him and know more of God daily. It seems more important to me than ever before in my life. I seek the Lord in.

- ✓ the holy scriptures,
- ✓ through the guidance of the Holy Spirit, and
- ✓ by joining my husband in doing Bible study.

There is much joy in seeking him *under every shade tree* that He provides for me, as well as in the beautiful truths of every hymn I play and sing.

As I seek more of God, His steadfast love is so evident in His daily care for all creation. God's love has given me salvation and an abundant life in His Spirit. His unconditional love is such a blessing as I turn to Him daily in the struggles of this life. This world can be so cruel, evil, and no fun sometimes. There are things in this world that I do not understand. Many distractions keep people from seeking and knowing the one true God. Yet our living God always wants people to seek Him, to know Him, and to worship Him. I sense His holiness and His power more and more every day in the little things of life, as well as the big stuff. He is God; He is my God!

YOUR THOUGHTS

✓ Why is it important to seek God?
✓ How do you think God wants us to seek Him?

_____

_____

_____

_____

_____

_____

_____

_____

_____

_____

GOD'S WORD

❖ *The LORD looks down from heaven on all mankind to see if there are any who understand, any who seek after God.* Psalm 14:2.

❖ *The LORD is good to those whose hope is in him, to the one who seeks him.* Lamentations 3:25

❖ *O God, you are my God, earnestly I seek you; I thirst for you, my whole being longs for you, in a dry and parched land where there is no water.* Psalm 63:1

❖ *And God made from one man every nation of mankind to live on the face of the earth, having determined allotted periods of time and boundaries of their dwelling place, that they should seek God and find him.* Acts 17:26-27

❖ *But may all who seek you rejoice and be glad in you, may those who long for your saving help always say, "Great is the LORD."* Psalm 40:16

HYMN FOR TODAY

O God You Are My God (David Strasser and Rich Mullins)
Seek Ye First (Karen Lafferty, 1972)

God, I thank You for the animals, who remind me how much You love and care for Your creation.

O h, the blessings I have always received by seeking and finding God early in the morning when my day is fresh and at its best! Early one morning, while sitting on the deck, I watched several young deer in the vacant lot behind our home. They were running and playing without a care in the world. They soon stopped to graze with the others and then went on their way. In a little while, one lone deer darted across the lot as fast as he could to catch up with the others. My other observations were of the three happy squirrels who live in our backyard, as well as the many birds.

My thoughts recalled the times during the past week when I had felt unsure about what was happening in our personal lives, as well as all the unrest in our country. Seeking the assurance that God is faithful in taking care of us in all situations is so essential. I remembered a poem that my friend Sarah had shared with me one evening when we were visiting on the phone. It is a beautifully embroidered verse that belonged to her sweet mother.

In 1859, Elizabeth Cheney penned the poem featured below. It is a strong message for us today!

Said the Robin to the Sparrow,
"I would really like to know,
Why these anxious human beings
Rush around and worry so."

Said the Sparrow to the Robin,
"Friend, I think that it must be,
That they have no heavenly Father,
Such as cares for you and me."

As we seek God and see Him in our surroundings, let us always have the assurance that God's eye is on us as we trust in Him. I hope to experience the same happiness and freedom as the animals that remind me of God's care.

YOUR THOUGHTS

✓ How do you seek God during all the chaos of our time?
✓ How have you depended on God's care?

_____

_____

_____

_____

_____

_____

_____

_____

_____

GOD'S WORD

❖ *In the morning, LORD, you hear my voice; in the morning, I lay my requests before you and wait expectantly.* Psalm 5:3

❖ *Look to the LORD and his strength; seek his face always.* I Chronicles 16:11

❖ *Blessed are those who keep his statutes and seek him with their whole heart.* Psalm 119:2

❖ *Jesus said, "Look at the birds of the air, they do not sow or reap or store away in barns, and yet your heavenly Father feeds them. Are you not much more valuable than they? Can anyone of you by worrying add a single hour to your life?"* Matthew 6:26-27

HYMN FOR TODAY

His Eye Is on the Sparrow (Civilla D. Martin,1905)

> *God, I acknowledge Your powerful plan for all Your creation while seeking You in my nighttime worship.*

Seeking more of God while sitting *under the shade tree* at nighttime is quite an experience and different from the daytime. On some evenings, I found myself outside enjoying a gentle breeze and the sounds of the night: insects, frogs, birds, and much more. The best nights were when there was a gorgeous full moon and the sky filled with stars. Oh, the wisdom of our God to know that we need light in the heavens at night!

Yes, the sights and sounds of nighttime display the power of creation, as only God can organize and create for His purpose. Even as the sounds seemed quite loud and noisy at times, I was reminded again of all creation praising God. It's a beautiful chorus, for sure! Indeed, all these creatures were thanking God for His provisions just as my husband and I continued to sing praises for giving us His beautiful creation here on the lake as well as provision for all our physical and spiritual needs not only during this time but for all the days of our lives.

All of God's creations praise Him just by their very existence and by being what God designed for them to be. It is such a beautiful thought to ponder God's creation and the plan God has for each part of it, including mankind. Oh, what a blessing to seek and enjoy God's presence in the beauty of His nighttime creation!

YOUR THOUGHTS

✓ How do you see God in His creation at night?
✓ How do you see all creation worshiping Him?

_____

_____

_____

_____

_____

_____

_____

_____

_____

_____

GOD'S WORD

❖ *And God said, "Let there be lights in the expanse of the sky to divide the day from the night and let them be for signs to mark seasons and for days and years. And let them be for lights in the expanse of the sky to give light upon the earth" And it was so. God made two great lights—the greater light to govern the day and the lesser light to govern the night. He also made the stars.* Genesis 1:14-16

❖ *Lift up your eyes and look to the heavens: Who created all these? He who brings out the starry hosts one by one and calls them each by name. Because of his great power and mighty strength, not one of them is missing.* Isaiah 40:26

❖ *God made the earth by his power; he founded the world by his wisdom and stretched out the heavens by his understanding.* Jeremiah 10:12

❖ *Praise the Lord. Praise the Lord from the heavens; praise him in the heights above. Praise him, all His angels, praise him, all his heavenly hosts. Praise him, sun and moon. Praise him all you shining stars. Praise him, you highest heavens, and you, waters above the skies. Let them praise the name of the LORD, for he*

commanded, and they were created, and he established them forever and ever."
Psalm 148:1-5

HYMNS FOR TODAY

 All Creatures of Our God and King (William H. Draper)
How Great Thou Art (Stuart K. Hine)

> *Dear Father in Heaven, I thank You for loving me so much that You sent Jesus to be my Lord and Savior.*

One morning, while communicating with my heavenly Father, I was thanking him for Jesus. Thinking about Jesus, who became my Savior, Lord, and Friend. God the Father loved us so much that He sent Jesus to earth to be a sacrifice for our sinful nature. Then Jesus' resurrected body arose to join the Father in Heaven. He then sent us the Holy Spirit to lead and guide us in our daily lives. I call Him friend because He is with me daily through the Holy Spirit.

A friend is someone who always listens and cares, and that is how I see Jesus. I talk with Him daily, all day long. Many days, I feel that He is the only friend on whom I can depend as I share life with my husband, who is going through his health problems.

Without my trusting in Jesus, I would not really know the Father and His gift of the Holy Spirit. Without Him, I would not have the joy of salvation and abundant life. Without Jesus, I do not know what my life would be. The first time I remember singing the hymn "What a Friend We Have in Jesus" was at a funeral when I was six years old. My beautiful fifteen-year-old cousin, Joyce, died of a ruptured appendix, and this song was sung at her funeral in a little country church in East Texas. On that day, I remember how much our family trusted in Jesus to give us hope and peace.

When thinking about Jesus being my friend, I began to think about my relationship with Him. Does Jesus see me as his friend? The word "obedience" came to my mind as I pondered how I show that I am Jesus' friend. I need to be aware of my obedience to Jesus daily to enjoy my relationship with Him genuinely. My love for my Savior and my obedience to His teachings and commandments show that I am His friend.

YOUR THOUGHTS

✓ What are some ways you see Jesus as your friend?

✓ What actions can you take to demonstrate your friendship with Jesus?

_____

_____

_____

_____

_____

_____

_____

_____

_____

GOD'S WORD

❖ *Jesus said, "Greater love has no one than this, that he lay down one's life for one's friends."* John 15:13

❖ *Jesus said, "You are my friends if you do what I command."* John 15:14

❖ *Those whom I love I rebuke and discipline. So be earnest and repent. Here I am! I stand at the door and knock. If anyone hears my voice and opens the door, I will come in and eat with that person, and they will be with me.* Revelation 3:19-20

❖ *Follow God's example, therefore, as dearly loved children and walk in the way of love, just as Christ loved us and gave himself up for us, as a fragrant offering and sacrifice to God.* Ephesians 5:1-2

❖ *We love because he first loved us.* 1 John 4:19

HYMNS FOR TODAY

 What a Friend We Have in Jesus (Joseph Scriven, 1855)
My Jesus, I Love Thee (William Featherston)

Heavenly Father, I am seeking Your comfort while hurting emotionally today. Thank You for blessing me through my friend.

My husband and I were happy and had always enjoyed our life together. We so appreciated God's love and care for us. But sometimes, I can become quite emotional while facing some tricky situations in life and seek God's comfort and guidance in those days.

On a Monday, I was experiencing loneliness and a heavy heart because I could not see family and friends in person. That day, I drove to the local pharmacy to get some needed items. Yes, I wore my mask!

I sat in my car for a while, parked *under a shade tree,* and called my long-time friend, Pat. She is always understanding. She knows my faith in God; we have experienced much together over the last fifty years. Pat listens—she prays with me and doesn't tell me what to do or bother me with many questions.

As we were having our phone visit, I noticed two younger ladies had driven up and were standing *under the shade tree,* talking and laughing. It appeared that they had their children in the cars with the AC turned on. It seemed as if they had not seen each other in a while and were enjoying their time together. This "shade tree" experience on that Monday reminded me that God often blesses us with His love and encouragement through a friend.

YOUR THOUGHTS

✓ Tell about times in your life when God encouraged you through a friend.

✓ What are some specific ways you see friends encouraging each other in the name of Jesus?

_____

_____

_____

_____

_____

_____

_____

_____

_____

_____

GOD'S WORD

❖ *Oil and perfume make the heart glad; the sweetness of a friend comes from the earnest of his counsel.* Proverbs 27:9

❖ *A friend loves at all times, and a brother is born for a time of adversity.* Proverbs 17:17

❖ *A man of many companions may come to ruin, but there is a friend who sticks closer than a brother.* Proverbs 18:24.

❖ *Therefore, encourage one another and build each other up just as you are doing.* I Thessalonians 5:11

HYMNS FOR TODAY

Blest Be the Tie (John Fawcett,1782)
Friends are Friends Forever (Michael W. Smith)

Outings during the pandemic were limited to early morning trips to the local pharmacy and the grocery store. The clerk at the pharmacy always recognized me, and we enjoyed a conversation every time. She was trying to go to other states to visit her children, but airline restrictions delayed her trips. I always wanted to give her an encouraging word.

The second week of August was my time to buy groceries for the month. The friendly lady who checked me out took charge of loading my cart and getting it all organized for me. She told me that her husband was recovering from back surgery, and she was trying to work and take care of him. My neighbor, Olga, was longing to see her adult son, who had been hospitalized for several weeks. My prayer life began to include these women and many more who were experiencing specific needs. Others I knew had lost loved ones to the virus or other medical conditions.

During the pandemic, my heart felt sadness for families who carried the burden of their need to be together and for those who cared for ill family members. I prayed for all not to become discouraged. I sensed anger in some people over the situations of life during those days. It was indeed a time for people to seek God and not turn away from Him. Even amid the twists and turns of my own life, I was blessed to reach out to others. For I knew that it was God doing it through me, and I give Him the praise and glory.

I noticed all the teenagers who worked at fast food restaurants and knew in my heart that this new way of life would be difficult for them. So, I started the habit of calling out their names when I went through the drive-through, telling them that I was a Christian and that I would be praying for them. I always got a smile, and a thank you from each one of them. I never asked them questions or put them on the spot. I just offered them a smile and a prayer. And I did pray for them, asking God to bless them and provide for all their needs. I also prayed that my words to them might inspire them to seek and know God.

Yes, there were so many concerns, burdens, and hurting people who needed encouragement filled with God's love. Sharing God's love through encouraging words was beneficial to others and lifted my spirits. My hope was that my prayers and words to others might be "throwing out a lifeline" to someone who truly needed it.

YOUR THOUGHTS

✓ What specific needs or burdens do you think people had then and have now?
✓ How do you think that God uses our words of encouragement?

_____

_____

_____

_____

_____

_____

_____

_____

_____

_____

GOD'S WORD

❖ *Cast your cares on the LORD, and He will sustain you. He will never let the righteous fall.* Psalm 55:22

❖ *Do not let any unwholesome talk come out of your mouths, but only what is helpful for building others up according to their needs that may benefit those who listen.* Ephesians 4:29.

❖ *See to it, brothers and sisters, that none of you has a sinful, unbelieving heart that turns away from the living God. But encourage one another daily so that none of you may be hardened by sin's deceitfulness. We have come to share in Christ if, indeed, we hold our original conviction firmly to the very end.* Hebrews 3:12-14

❖ *The mouth of the righteous is a fountain of life, but violence overwhelms the mouth of the wicked.* Proverbs 10:11

❖ *Carry each other's burdens, and in this way, you will fulfill the law of Christ.* Galatians 6:2

HYMNS FOR TODAY

People Need the Lord (Greg Nelson and Phil McHugh,1983)

Throw Out the Lifeline (Edward S. Ufford,1888)

God, help us to distance ourselves from things that will harm our witness of You in our lives.

During 2020 and 2021, social distancing became the way of life for most of us, apparently to protect us from the virus. Many people were very dedicated to following the guidelines, while others thought distancing was unimportant. Thinking about this, I thought about God's plan for social distancing in our Christian walk. Throughout our lifetime, most of us have read and understood the Bible teachings about the importance of Christians distancing from the worldly things in our midst that will harm us.

If we do not keep ourselves away from them, we are affected mentally and physically, which can sometimes bring heartache and destruction to our lives. Getting so closely involved in things that are not pleasing to God keeps us from seeing and knowing His best for us. Yet some people seem to go along with life and want to have fun and enjoy whatever comes their way, especially in social situations. The focus for many people in the 21st century seems to be *self, what I want, my rights, and nothing will harm me.*

Learning to say "no" to some things is essential. Years ago, I heard my husband make a speech at an end-of-the-year dinner for teachers in our school district. He pointed out the fact that teachers had spent the year telling students to "just say no." He challenged them to make sure the next year students would be given plenty of opportunities to say "yes" to things that would help build a good character and a successful life. Remembering this, I am assured that saying "yes" to Biblical teachings and listening to the voice of God in our lives can help us distance ourselves from the evils of this world. And what a witness it is of our God living in us!

YOUR THOUGHTS

- ✓ During the pandemic, did you have difficulty with social distancing?
- ✓ Have you witnessed or personally experienced the failure of distancing from Satan's temptations? What were the results?
- ✓ How do we, as Christians, keep our distance from ungodly things?

_____

_____

_____

_____

_____

_____

_____

_____

_____

_____

GOD'S WORD

- ❖ *Do not be misled. "Bad company corrupts good character.* I Corinthians 15:33

- ❖ *A dishonest man spreads strife, and a gossip separates close friends.* Proverbs 16:28

- ❖ *The righteous choose his friends carefully, but the way of the wicked leads them astray.* Proverbs 12:26

- ❖ *Submit yourselves, then, to God. Resist the devil, and he will flee from you. Come near to God, and He will come near to you.* James 4:7-8

❖ *Dear friends, I urge you, as foreigners and exiles, to abstain from sinful desires which wages war against your soul. Live such good lives among the pagans that, though they accuse you of doing wrong, they may see your good deeds and glorify God on the day he visits us.* I Peter 2:11-12

❖ *I urge you, brothers and sisters, in view of God's mercy, to offer your bodies as a living sacrifice, holy and pleasing to God—that is your true and proper worship. Do not conform to the pattern of this world, but be transformed by the renewing of your mind. Then, you will be able to test and approve what God's will is—his good, pleasing, and perfect will.* Romans 12:1-2

HYMNS FOR TODAY:

I Surrender All (Judson W. Van de Venter, 1896)
O Jesus, I Have Promised (John E. Bode, 1888)

One day, while sitting *under the shade tree,* I was reminded of the attack on the United States on September 11, 2001. What a horrific event! Such a tragedy for the people of New York City and our entire country. People were crying out to God for help.

I recall that there were reports that places of worship in America were filled with grieving, praying people on the following Sunday. Yes, people appeared to need God, so praying and worshiping God seemed necessary for a few weeks. Then, it was reported that the number of worshipers began to dwindle. How quickly a society can turn away from God! It is my prayer that we will never forget the faith of our founding fathers, who built our nation with a Biblical foundation and teach it to all generations.

In 2020, the enemy was COVID-19, which attacked the entire world, including many of our large cities and across the nation. In fact, it was touching every area in our country. People were crying and praying; however, this time, the places of worship had to close their doors. Witnessing that event made me contemplate God's sovereignty and how His power manifests in our lives during challenging moments. I pondered three things:

✓ Were we, as believers, spending time individually in prayer and worship?
✓ Was our focus on God or perhaps more on the problems brought on by the pandemic?
✓ Were we praying for physical and spiritual healing for people in our communities?

Yes, there was the necessity for God's people to gather for times of praying for our nation, but it truly must begin in the individual hearts of His people, keeping in close fellowship with their Lord.

God will always show His love and continue living through His people, as well as wanting unbelievers to seek and find Him. I thought about what might happen in our churches when believers could finally return to worshiping together. If we truly seek and worship Him, what will our powerful sovereign God do in our midst and through us?

YOUR THOUGHTS

✓ What do you think people learned about prayer and worship during those times?

_____

_____

_____

_____

_____

_____

_____

_____

_____

_____

GOD'S WORD

❖ *If my people who are called by my name will humble themselves and pray and seek my face and turn from their wicked ways, then I will hear from heaven, and I will forgive their sin and will heal their land.* 2 Chronicles 7:14

❖ *Come let us bow down in worship, let us kneel before the LORD our Maker; for he is our God and we are the people of his pasture, and the flock under his care.* Psalm 95:6

❖ *Therefore, confess your sins to each other and pray for each other so that you may be healed. The prayer of a righteous person is powerful and effective.* James 5:16

❖ *Jesus said, "For where two or three gather in my name, there I am with them. "* Matthew 18:20

❖ *The believers devoted themselves to the apostles' teachings and to fellowship, to the breaking of bread and prayer. Everyone was filled with awe at the many wonders and signs performed by the apostles. And the Lord added to their number daily those who were being saved.* Acts 2:42-43, 47

HYMNS FOR TODAY

If My People Will Pray (Jimmy Owens, 1973)
Close to Thee (Fanny Crosby, 1874)

EXPERIENCING GOD IN SPIRITUAL HEALING

God, forgive us for making our desire for material things more important than Spiritual needs. Help us to see what indeed honors You.

One interesting thing about the COVID pandemic, with everyone staying at home, is that some people began to see how much their lives depended on material things. Yes, many of those things were nonessential, and there was a time when people could shop for only "essential" items. Perhaps it was a time when we all learned what should be most important in our lives.

Almost daily, I saw on local social media sites people purging and putting things by their curbs to give away for "free." It is easy in our society in America to be collectors of various things, and many businesses often entice us to purchase things that we probably don't need. We buy items, use them briefly, and then store them in our homes. I have known some women with huge closets of clothes and shoes, and they continually purchase more.

Just think about all the "things" that men and women consider essential purchases in their lives. I also noticed from conversations and social media that when stores began to reopen, some people rushed out to purchase more "things" that probably were not essential to their lives. According to some, the act of shopping and acquiring possessions can provide a feeling of satisfaction.

Oh, the thoughts that flooded my mind! Has our society become so addicted to buying and having so much in material things? Does going out on a shopping spree give us more pleasure than spending time with God in His Word or time ministering to others as God leads? Are we, as believers, following the teachings of Jesus? Do we depend on material things to give us happiness and satisfaction in life?

YOUR THOUGHTS

✓ Did you learn anything about your "possessions" during the pandemic?
✓ How has owning those "things" affected your life?

_____

_____

_____

_____

_____

_____

_____

_____

_____

GOD'S WORD

❖ *Then he said to them, "Watch out! Be on your guard against all kinds of greed; life does not consist in an abundance of possessions."* Luke 12:15

❖ *Jesus said, "Do not store up for yourselves treasures on earth, where moths and vermin destroy and where thieves break in and steal. But store up for yourselves treasures in heaven, where moths and vermin do not destroy and where thieves do not break in and steal. For where your treasure is, there your heart will be also."* Matthew 6:19-21

❖ *But godliness with contentment is great gain. For we brought nothing into this world, and we can take nothing out of it. But if we have food and clothing, we will be content with that.* I Timothy 6:6-8

❖ *I consider everything a loss because of the surpassing worth of knowing Christ Jesus, my Lord, for whose sake I have lost all things.* Philippians 3:8

HYMNS FOR TODAY

I'd Rather Have Jesus (Rhea F. Miller-1922)
I'll Worship Only at the Feet of Jesus (Bill Gaither)

Jesus, I thank You for living and loving through Your Church during these difficult days. I pray that our deeds will honor You.

At times, people experienced a period of total isolation from others except those in their immediate family. In most areas, the opportunity to be with fellow Christians physically at a church building was *not* happening. So, how could the church be the church? Did the church survive? Again, we were reminded that the church is not a building but a body of believers who continue to worship God and allow his Spirit to work through them all over the world. God's people worshiped in their homes and prayed daily during this time.

I saw photos of pastors praying together with the President at the White House. Some churches ministered in various ways to their communities. Some people in their neighborhoods reached out to others, if possible, and several churches presented gift baskets for healthcare workers. Christians were praying and encouraging others daily through phone calls, texts, or emails. Many Christians were praying, especially for our government leaders and for those making decisions about health care.

The church survives because Christians continue to let the Holy Spirit live and love through them. The Spirit of our "living" God is alive and well! Even when I saw some of the media be so hostile and almost mocking God, I knew the church was faithful because God is always faithful. Yes, the people of God always seem to rise in service to the King of Kings as the church triumphs over the evils of these times.

YOUR THOUGHTS

- ✓ What were some of the obstacles the church had to face?
- ✓ How were believers able to be strong during this time?
- ✓ Name some ways you saw the church honoring God.

_____

_____

_____

_____

_____

_____

_____

_____

_____

_____

GOD'S WORD

- ❖ *A generous person will prosper; whoever refreshes others will be refreshed.* Proverbs 11:25

- ❖ *What good is it, my brothers and sisters, if someone claims to have faith but has no deeds? You see, a person is considered righteous by what they do and not by faith alone.* James 2:14, 24

- ❖ *Devote yourselves to prayer, being watchful and thankful.* Colossians 4:2

- ❖ *May God himself, the God of peace, sanctify you through and through. May your whole spirit, soul, and body be kept blameless at the coming of our Lord Jesus Christ. The one who calls you is faithful, and he will do it.* I Thessalonians 5:23-24

❖ *The Lord is faithful. He will strengthen you and protect you from the evil one.*
  2 Thessalonians 3:3

HYMNS FOR TODAY

The Church Triumphant (William and Gloria Gaither)
Rise Up, O Men of God (William P. Merrill,1911)

Lord, I praise You for the provisions of modern technology. I am most grateful for our assurance in Your steadfast love for us.

Since the beginning of time, God has provided mankind the mind and hands to create things to be used in our life on earth. It is so interesting to see how such innovation has progressed in time to what humans enjoy today in modern technology. Yes, it became so vital in our lives, especially during the pandemic, which we experienced from 2020 to 2021.

However, one of the frustrations during the pandemic was the periodic loss of technology on which we have become so dependent in the 21st century. Several days, Max and I experienced the loss of internet and cable television. Even though we missed some Zoom life groups and some church services, we were okay. Our landline and cell phones worked, for which we were grateful. I thought about what communication is most important to us. Having my husband to talk with all day was a blessing. Talking and texting with family and friends, as well as with medical facilities, was vital.

But Max and I were most grateful for our uninterrupted communication with God, who is a most essential part of our life. Talking and listening to God does not require modern technology. It is only through the power of the Holy Spirit that we communicate with God. And so, we experienced many blessings in our talks with Him! We were filled with peace and comfort as we listened to God mainly through his Holy Scriptures. In our daily living, we continued to sing praises to our Savior all day long with a blessed assurance of His great mercy and love for us.

YOUR THOUGHTS

✓ How crucial is technology to you?

✓ How do you see technology being used to honor God?

✓ Who do you communicate with most during your day?

_____

_____

_____

_____

_____

_____

_____

_____

GOD'S WORD

❖ _And the LORD has filled him with the Spirit of God, with wisdom, with understanding, with knowledge and all kinds of skills._ Exodus 35:31

❖ _Praise be to the name of God for ever and ever; wisdom and power are his._ Daniel 2:20

❖ _And I am convinced that nothing will ever separate us from God's love. Neither death nor life, neither angels nor demons, neither the present nor the future, not any powers. No power in the sky above or in the earth below, nor anything in all creation will ever be able to separate us from the love of God that is in Christ Jesus our Lord._ Romans 8:38-39

HYMNS FOR TODAY

 Blessed Assurance (Fanny Crosby)

> *Thank you, God, for Your Holy Scriptures to help us know You and Your love for us.*

My husband and I have always read and studied God's Holy Word. Max read the Bible with our family as our children were growing up. I remember one time when our son was about ten years of age; he asked his dad a question while we were riding in the car. When we arrived home, my husband opened his Bible and read scriptures to answer Greg's question. What a blessing!

My husband taught adults on Sunday mornings for many years. For the last couple of years, he asked our Sunday morning Bible study group to repeat this verse every week:

> *Love the LORD your God with all your heart, with all your soul,*
> *with your mind and with all your strength.*
> *And love your neighbor as yourself.* Mark 12:30

All of us in the group knew that Max valued reading and studying the Bible, and it was one way he demonstrated his love of God.

Hopefully, a person who seeks God in His Holy Word and sees His messages for our daily lives will most likely make Bible reading a vital part of his or her life. So, personal Bible study continued to be important to us and gave us much strength and guidance during the months of COVID-19 isolation. I prayed that more people who were hurting during this challenging time in our lives would seek God through the scriptures.

YOUR THOUGHTS

✓ How has studying the Bible helped you?
✓ Do you have a favorite book in the Bible or a favorite scripture?

_____

_____

_____

_____

_____

_____

_____

_____

_____

GOD'S WORD

❖ *Your word is a lamp for my feet, a light on my path.* Psalm 119:105

❖ *Jesus answered, "It is written: Man shall not live by bread alone, but on every word that comes from the mouth of God."* Matthew 4:4

❖ *All Scripture is God-breathed and useful for teaching, rebuking, correcting, and training in righteousness, so that the servant of God may be thoroughly equipped to every good work.* 2 Timothy 3:16-17

❖ *For everything that was written in the past was written to teach us so that through the endurance taught in the Scriptures and the encouragement they provide, we might have hope.* Romans 15:4

HYMNS FOR TODAY

Holy Bible, Book Divine (John Burton,1803)

Jesus Loves Me (Anna Bartlett Warner,1859)

Thank you, Heavenly Father, for our blood, which is physically our lifeline, and for the blood of Jesus, who was sacrificed for our spiritual lifeline.

On my birthday in April 2020, once again I sat in the car *under the shade tree* for over three hours while my husband went in alone for a bone marrow biopsy. On that day, I received many texts and calls expressing concern for my husband, along with birthday greetings for myself.

Periodically, my husband needed to have blood transfusions because his bone marrow did not make the blood he needed. So often, when thinking about his blood disease while he was receiving blood transfusions, I wondered about the anonymous person who had donated the blood so that it could help my husband. For many years, Max had been very dedicated to giving the gift of his own blood to those in need. Little did we know that years later, he would be the recipient of blood donations. Donations of blood save lives. Yes, donating blood is life-giving, but not a great human sacrifice.

Being grateful for the blood transfusions that my husband received, I often thought about how the sacrificial shed blood of Jesus saves our lives from a sinful nature and unites us with the Father. Many years ago, our family attended the opening of the Biblical Arts Center in Dallas. My husband was so entranced by one art piece of Christ with the crown of thorns that he purchased it. As we moved from place to place, that artwork has always gone with us and been placed where we could see it daily. Such a reminder of the sacrificial blood for our sins to give us life, as well as the need to be spiritually healed by the power of the blood of Jesus.

Receiving blood transfusions can increase energy and healing here on Earth. Yet it is vital to our spiritual life here on earth for each of us to come to repentance and acceptance of the blood of Jesus, which forgives mankind from our sins. With that decision, we can live a life filled with His Spirit and receive the promise of eternal life with the Father. I often say," Thank You, Jesus, for Your blood."

YOUR THOUGHTS

✓ How does accepting the blood of Jesus make a difference in your life, especially during challenging times?

✓ Do you need to share with someone who has not accepted Jesus as their Savior?

_____

_____

_____

_____

_____

_____

_____

_____

_____

_____

GOD'S WORD

❖ *Jesus said, "This is my blood of the covenant, which is poured out for many for the forgiveness of sins."* Matthew 26:28

❖ *For God so loved the world that he gave his one and only Son, that whoever believes in him shall not perish but have eternal life.* John 3:16

* ❖ *In Christ, we have redemption through his blood, the forgiveness of sins, in accordance with the riches of God's grace that he lavished on us.* Ephesians 1:7

* ❖ *God demonstrates His love for us in this: while we were still sinners, Christ died for us.* Ephesians 5:8

* ❖ *He himself bore our sins" in his body on the cross. so that we might die to sins and live for righteousness; "by his wounds you are healed." For, "you were like sheep gone astray," but now you have returned to the Shepherd and Overseer of your souls."* I Peter 2:24-25

HYMNS FOR TODAY

Blessed Redeemer (Avis B. Christiansen,1920)

The Blood Will Never Lose Its Power (Andraé Crouch,1962)

Just As I Am (Charlotte Elliott, 1836)

Thank You, Father, for the privilege of being in the Body of Christ through His shed blood.

One day, *under the shade tree*, while communicating with my Heavenly Father, I began to focus on the word "body." When Max and I first met, he was athletic and had a big and muscular body. I watched him coach high school athletes for many years. When he retired, he had been a coach for thirty-seven years. However, over the past few years, I have seen his robust and healthy body go down physically. Age and diseases cause our bodies to decline physically. Yet, it is in our frail earthly bodies that God displays his glorious Spirit as we allow. Our bodies weaken, but His Spirit continues to live in us to honor Him and is used in His body of believers.

God the Father sent Jesus with a physical body to live, teach, and do the work of the Father. He became the sacrifice for our sin on the cross, then arose from death and lives eternally. When we become a believer and a follower of Jesus, we are part of the Body of Christ, partaking in His death and resurrection. We are blessed to share in His inheritance. The Body of Christ must be filled with His Spirit that shows the world the power of a Heavenly Father's great love for mankind and the presence of the living God whom we worship.

As our earthly bodies die, the Spirit in us will be with God. As Christians, we are the Body of Christ, allowing Jesus to do His work through us as the church. I am thankful that the Body of Christ will live forever. As believers on this earth, we experience such a "Sweet Spirit" when we gather to worship and to serve our exalted Lord and Savior.

YOUR THOUGHTS

✓ How do you describe the physical body and spiritual body?
✓ What does it mean for you to be in the Body of Christ?

_____

_____

_____

_____

_____

_____

_____

_____

_____

GOD'S WORD

❖ *You, however, are not in the realm of the flesh but are in the realm of the Spirit: if indeed the Spirit of God lives in you. And if anyone does not have the Spirit of Christ, they do not belong to Christ. But if Christ is in you then even though your body is subject to death because of sin, the Spirit gives life because of righteousness.* Romans 8:9-10

❖ *For by the grace given to me, I say to every one of you. Do not think of yourself more highly than you ought, but rather think of yourself with sober judgment in accordance with the faith God has distributed to each of you. For just as each of us has one body with many members, and these members do not have the same function, so in Christ we, though many, form one body, and each member belongs to all the others.* Romans 12:3-5

❖ *And God placed all things under Jesus Christ's feet and appointed him to be head over the church, which is his body, the fullness of him who fills everything in every way.* Ephesians 1:22-23

❖ *Instead, speaking the truth in love, we will grow to become in every respect the mature body of him who is the head, that is, Christ. From Him, the whole body, joined and held together by every supporting ligament, grows, and builds itself up in love, as each part does its work.* Ephesians 4:15-16

❖ *So Christ himself gave the apostles, the prophets, the evangelists, the pastors and teachers to equip His people for works of service, so that the body of Christ may be built up until we all reach unity in the faith and the knowledge of the Son of God become mature, attaining the full measure of the fullness of Christ.* Ephesians 4:11-13

HYMNS FOR TODAY

We Are the Body of Christ (Scott W. Brown and David Hampton)
Sweet, Sweet Spirit (Doris Akers,1962)

> *Father in heaven, I am so grateful for the refreshing rain today and for the showers of blessing that You send to us.*

I was sitting in the parking lot at the hospital, waiting for my husband. There was no shade tree for me on that day because it was a day to enjoy a refreshing rain, which cooled off our hot temperatures here in Texas. My thoughts were recalling the words of the old hymn "Showers of Blessing" as I appreciated the nice, steady rain.

In recent days, we had experienced times of uncertainty with my husband's health issues and the many days spent on medical appointments. Yet, in those days, Max and I often spoke of the blessings of our lives. Here are some things we did to continue to be mindful of God's hand on own lives:

- ✓ We talked of the blessings of our careers and the lives that had touched us.
- ✓ We continued to see how God blesses us by providing us with a retirement income that provides shelter, food, and the necessities of life.
- ✓ We were so appreciative of the blessings of such loving care at the Houston Methodist and the medicines that gave us continued life together during this surreal time in our world.
- ✓ We saw God caring for us through family members and faithful friends. Yes, we counted our blessings.
- ✓ We lived each day thanking God for the many physical blessings of our lives, and we were more grateful for our spiritual blessings.
- ✓ We thanked God for our salvation through the love, grace, and sacrifice of our Savior.

- ✓ We continued to live daily, blessed in a relationship with our living Lord, who gives us joy, peace, and the promise of life in heaven.
- ✓ We were fortunate to be living in the presence of our Lord and we were enjoying all His blessings.

Even though the facts about my husband's medical condition filled us with uncertainty, we trusted God and thanked Him for His blessings. I believe that just as the rain can refresh our earth, our acknowledgment of God's blessings can be a spiritual renewal, refreshing our hearts with His steadfast love.

YOUR THOUGIITS

- ✓ What were some of your "showers of blessing" during the pandemic or in recent days?
- ✓ What did you learn about God in those blessings?

_____

_____

_____

_____

_____

_____

_____

_____

_____

_____

GOD'S WORD

❖ *The LORD bless you and keep you; the Lord make His face shine upon you and be gracious to you. The LORD turn his face toward you and give you peace.* Numbers 6:24-26

❖ *You gave abundant showers, O God; You refreshed your weary inheritance.* Psalm 68:9

❖ *I will send down showers in season; there will be showers of blessing.* Ezekiel 34:26

❖ *For I will pour water on the thirsty land, and streams on the dry ground; I will pour out my Spirit on your offspring, and my blessing on your descendants.* Isaiah 44:3

❖ *Praise be to the God and Father of our Lord Jesus Christ, who has blessed us in the heavenly realms with every spiritual blessing in Christ.* Ephesians 1:3

❖ *God is able to bless you abundantly, so that in all things at all times, having all that you need, you will abound in every good work.* 2 Corinthians 9:8

HYMNS FOR TODAY

Showers of Blessing (D. W. Whittle, 1883)
Count Your Blessings (Johnson Oatman, Jr., 1897)

God, I need my heart to know Your peace in these days of uncertainty with health issues.

During the pandemic, my husband was diagnosed with bladder cancer. For over a year, he had been receiving treatments for a blood disease. In our consultations with hematologists and his urologist, we learned he could not have surgery or any chemotherapy treatments for bladder cancer because of the blood disease and low blood counts. During a Friday afternoon phone conference, the hematologist suggested that the only therapy for survival of the blood disease would be for him to be admitted into the downtown Houston Methodist Hospital.

Our son and I would drive Max to the front door for him to go in alone and spend a week receiving treatments that would be pretty harsh on his body. The policy was "no visitors" at any time because of the COVID restrictions. My husband was ready to do this. We were overly concerned about what such a week would be like for him, so we spent the weekend praying for God's will to be done. The doctor planned to call us on Monday to set up the day and time for this.

Well, we waited all day, and then at about four o'clock on Monday afternoon, we finally received the call. The two hematologists had discussed Max's situation and decided that it would not be suitable for him to be in the hospital. They prescribed two more medicines for him to take in pill form at home for two months. We were both very relieved and pleased with this decision.

My husband had always lived with a strong faith in God. I had watched him read and study GOD'S WORD for many years, so Max knew in whom he believed. His favorite Bible verses were about the peace that God gives us. My husband's trust in God's peace was such an encouragement to me, as well as others who knew him. His faith and easy-going personality made it a joy to share life with him. We were so blessed!

YOUR THOUGHTS

✓ What were some of your stressful experiences during the pandemic time or a low time in your life?

✓ Have you seen God give you peace in a stressful or uncertain situation?

_____

_____

_____

_____

_____

_____

_____

_____

_____

GOD'S WORD

❖ *So, fear not for I am with you, be not dismayed, for I am your God, I will strengthen you and help you. I will uphold you with my righteous right hand.* Isaiah 41:10

❖ *You keep in perfect peace those whose minds are steadfast because they trust in You.* Isaiah 26:3

❖ *Jesus said, "I have told you these things, so that in me you may have peace. In the world, you will have troubles. But take heart! I have overcome the world."* John 16:33

❖ *"Have faith in God," Jesus answered.* Mark 11:22

HYMNS FOR TODAY

Have Faith in God (May Agnew Stephens, 1897)
Thou Wilt Keep Him in Perfect Peace (Anonymous)

SEEING GOD IN RESTING, REFLECTING, AND TRUSTING

Lord, I thank You for Your provision of rest when I am so tired on some of these unsettled days.

While my husband and I were dealing with his bladder cancer, we spent a lot of time anxiously waiting for updates from urologists and hematologists. Expecting calls on certain days proved to be times of frustration and uncertainty. The calls did not come at the scheduled times. Despite knowing that the doctors had many patients and responsibilities, we remained calm and understanding. We never knew what a conversation with a doctor would give us. My husband always exhibited so much more patience than I did, even as I knew it was always in God's timing.

On one such day, while becoming so weary of waiting for a call, I decided to take a nap. A couple of hours later, as soon as I awoke, the call came. God had provided a physical rest for me instead of two more hours of waiting for a call that we desperately needed. The call was a good one and gave us some answers that we wanted to hear.

Physical rest and resting in the presence and guidance of God are both so essential in our lives. We continued to grasp the value of "resting" in the love and peace of our Heavenly Father.

YOUR THOUGHTS

✓ How is your physical rest?
✓ How do we, as believers, rest in Him daily?
✓ What results from truly resting in God?

_____

_____

_____

_____

_____

_____

_____

_____

_____

GOD'S WORD

❖ *The heavens and the earth were completed in all their vast array. By the seventh day, God had finished the work he had been doing, so on the seventh day, he rested from all his work.* Genesis 2:1-2

❖ *For in six days the LORD made the heavens and the earth, the sea, and all that is in them, but he rested on the seventh day. Therefore, the LORD blessed the Sabbath day and made it holy.* Exodus 20:11

❖ *When you lie down, you will not be afraid. When you lie down, your sleep will be sweet.* Proverbs 3:24

❖ *I will lie down and sleep in peace, for you alone, O LORD, make me dwell in safety.* Psalm 4:8

❖ *Jesus said, "Come to me, all who are weary and burdened, and I will give you rest."* Matthew 11:28

HYMNS FOR TODAY

 Near to the Heart of God (Cleland B. McAfee, 1903)

> *Thank you, God, for precious memories of our mothers and grandmothers.*

Mother's Day in May 2020 was particularly special. On that day, our son drove my husband and me to take red flowers to the gravesite of Max's mother in Magnolia, Texas. We cherish her memory as a lovely Christian lady who enjoyed life with much kindness and laughter. And such a blessing to have her as mother, mother-in-law, and grandmother for our children!

We then spent over an hour sitting outside in the front yard of our dear friend, Celeste, fondly called Max's "second Mom," who was 100 years old. Yes, we did social distancing with a small shade tree nearby with a birdfeeder, and we enjoyed seeing lots of birds come by while we were there. We also visited with her daughter-in law, whose husband had been Max's best friend during his teenage years. My husband had always enjoyed being in the Graves' home, where he felt loved and truly a part of the family.

Celeste continues to live in her home with her big dog and is a pretty, talented lady. We always appreciate her many fun stories sprinkled with words of wisdom. I admire the way she has touched so many lives through her faith in God, as he has been so evident in her life. We have always had so much fun with her.

Getting out of the house was so good for us that day since my husband's only other outings had been to medical appointments. Celeste was so happy that we had spent time with her, and it was perfect for Max to spend time with her. We then went home and enjoyed FaceTime with our daughter and her family, who live in California. I am so grateful for technology. It was a fun and blessed Mother's Day for sure.

YOUR THOUGHTS

✓ How did you spend Mother's Day during the lockdown?

✓ Does the influence or memory of a mother or grandmother help you get through the difficult times in your life?

_____

_____

_____

_____

_____

_____

_____

_____

_____

GOD'S WORD

❖ *Listen, my son, to your father's instructions and do not forsake your mother's teaching. They are a garland to grace your head and a chain to adorn your neck.* Proverbs 1:8-9

❖ *Whoever spares the rod hates their children, but the one who loves their children is careful to discipline them.* Proverbs 13:24

❖ *Charm is deceptive, and beauty is fleeting; but a woman who fears the LORD is to be praised.* Proverbs 31: 30

❖ *Likewise, teach the older women are to be reverent in the way they live not to be slanderers or addicted to much wine, but to teach what is good.* Titus 2:3

❖ *Be kind one to another, tenderhearted, forgiving one another, as Christ forgave you.* Ephesians 4:32

HYMNS FOR TODAY

 God, Give Us Christian Homes (Baylus B. McKinney)

> *I thank You, God, for family. We are especially grateful for our son who takes care of our needs.*

The pandemic underscored the significance of family like never before. Our son, who travels, flew in from Arizona the second week of March to spend a week with us. We were so thankful he could accompany us to an important consultation with Max's hematologist. He then traveled back to Texas in April.

Due to the lockdowns and his dad's illness, our son moved closer to us to assist with our needs. He came over every day after his work, which he did remotely. He would bring groceries or whatever we needed, while also taking care of our yard. And the best part of all was the time we spent with him after dinner in the evenings. He and his dad enjoyed watching old Western movies and baseball games. He would always join us for any phone conferences we had with Max's medical team.

Our son usually spends his summers in the mountains, where it is cooler, so we were grateful for his decision to be with us during the hot summer months. We appreciated all his support during this crucial time in our lives and saw God blessing our time together.

YOUR THOUGHTS

✓ How did your family help each other during the pandemic?
✓ To what other family units do you belong?

_____

_____

_____

_____

_____

_____

_____

_____

_____

_____

GOD'S WORD

❖ *Honor your father and your mother, so that you may live long in the land the LORD your God is giving you.* Exodus 20:12

❖ *Children are a heritage from the LORD, offspring a reward for him.* Psalm 127:3

❖ *Train a child up in the way he should go and when he is old, he will not turn from it.* Proverbs 22:6

❖ *Anyone who does not provide for their relatives, and especially for their own household, has denied the faith and is worse than an unbeliever.* I Timothy 5:8

HYMNS FOR TODAY

Happy the Home When God Is There (Henry Ware, 1846)

Heavenly Father, thank You for Your
awesome presence in the quietness
of this hour.

On a beautiful May day, I sat in the car *under a shade tree* at Houston Methodist. Once again, I felt a strong desire to dive into the Word and hear from God. So, after one phone call to my sister, who lives in East Texas, I did a lot of praying and reading the Bible while listening to the Father.

There was no music playing. I was just caught up in the calmness and quietness, focusing totally on what God had for me during that time. What a fantastic experience to have so much peace in the presence of my living God and to be totally unaware of any distractions!

When my husband came out to the car after almost two hours in the Infusion Center, he looked relieved and showed me the results of his blood test. We were both delighted that some of his blood count numbers had increased, and he would not need a blood transfusion this time.

My time alone with God in the middle of a parking lot with a noisy freeway behind me had indeed given me what I needed for my time of isolation in the car. My sanctuary became a time to focus only on God and His Holiness and to be fully enveloped in His loving care. I thank God for His presence in my quiet time and His presence with us as my husband happily drove us home that day.

YOUR THOUGHTS

✓ Can you share one of your experiences of being totally in the presence of God?
✓ What did you learn during that experience about God, or how were you blessed?

_____

_____

_____

_____

_____

_____

_____

_____

_____

GOD'S WORD

❖ *Jesus said, "Yet a time is coming and has now come when the true worshipers will worship the Father in the Spirit and in truth, for they are the kind of worshipers the Father seeks. God is spirit, and his worshipers must worship in the Spirit and in truth."* John 4:23-24

❖ *Worship the LORD in the splendor of his holiness, tremble before him, all the earth.* Psalm 96:9

❖ *Jesus answered, "It is written: 'Worship the Lord your God and serve him only.' "* Luke 4:8

❖ *Humble yourselves before the Lord, and He will lift you up.* James 4:10

HYMNS FOR TODAY

Breathe on Me, Breath of God (Edwin Hatch, 1878)

Spirit of the Living God (Daniel Iverson, 1926)

Dear God, I praise You for the assurance of
Your watchful care over us in all our days.

My husband and I were confined indoors for several months to protect ourselves, particularly my husband, from the virus. But sometimes, getting out to ride around became essential. Calling on God to keep us safe was so important. I was determined not to become paranoid of any dangers.

At first, when my husband would go out alone, I was pretty concerned because if he were in an accident, he would go alone to the hospital. Or if he were to get the virus, it would be so bad for him. Max went out only once or twice a week to go to the nearby store to buy a newspaper. He always wore a mask and gloves. One day I heard him tell someone in a phone conversation that he was being careful not to get the virus because he did not want to bring it home and then I become sick with it. All the while, I was so concerned about him and yet he was also worried about my health.

When Max realized he needed to leave the house, trusting God for his protection in every situation became crucial. I understood that by allowing my husband some independence, I was showing my love and respect for him. It was also a way of honoring our Heavenly Father, who had so lovingly cared for us through our fifty years of marriage. I found comfort in knowing that God would protect and care for us throughout our lives.

YOUR THOUGHTS

✓ What are some situations in which you had to depend entirely on God's protection for your loved ones?
✓ What are some ways people show love and respect for their loved ones?

_____

_____

_____

_____

_____

_____

_____

_____

GOD'S WORD

❖ *The angel of the LORD encamps around those who fear him, and he delivers them.* Psalm 34:7

❖ *The LORD will keep you from all harm—He will watch over your life; the LORD will watch over your coming and going both now and forevermore.*
Psalm 121:7-8

❖ *Do nothing out of selfish ambition or vain conceit. Rather, in humility value others above yourselves, not looking to your own interests but each of you to the interests of others.* Philippians 2:3-4

❖ *Love is patient. Love is kind. It does not envy, it does not boast, it is not proud.*
I Corinthians 13:4

HYMNS FOR TODAY

 God of All My Days (Mark Hall and Jason Ingram)

I am so grateful for Jesus, the Light of the world. My prayer is for believers to reflect that Light to others in this world of darkness.

There were always many restrictions at medical facilities because of the increasing spread of the virus. During my doctor's appointment on June 1, I had to wait in my car until the receptionist texted me to come inside. While sitting there in front of a large window, all I could see was the reflection of the trees on the other side of the parking lot.

I thought about how our eyes can see reflections because the glass in the window mirrors the image with the light rays. So, to reflect an image, there must be a physical light. If I were sitting in total darkness, I would not see the image reflected.

Immediately, I thought about the fact that when we repent of our sinful nature and accept Jesus, who is the Light of the world, we are filled with his Spiritual Light that enables us humbly to reflect the character of God. In Him, we walk in the light and not the darkness.

The word "reflections" was stuck in my thoughts. I began thinking of how the things I have learned throughout my life, especially while sitting *under the shade trees,* are reflected in my life. Most of the time, we are unaware of what our lives reflect in the world. What am I reflecting to others in my time of struggles, insecurities, and sad times? Am I reflecting God's love and his faithfulness to others? Do others see the joy and peace in my life that comes only from my relationship with the Father through the shed blood of Jesus? My prayer is that God is reflected in my daily life, bringing not only honor and glory to the Father, but also a witness and encouragement to others.

Yes, we must live daily in the awareness that Jesus, the Spiritual Light of the world, is living in us and enables us to reflect who He is to a world of darkness. That Light can be evident in all we say and do in faith and through the power of the Holy Spirit.

YOUR THOUGHTS

✓ Think about how God is reflected in our attitudes, our relationships, and even in all our daily activities.

✓ Can you name some specific Godly reflections that you have seen in other people that proved to be inspirational to you?

_____

_____

_____

_____

_____

_____

_____

_____

_____

_____

GOD'S WORD

❖ *As water reflects the face, one's life reflects the heart.* Proverbs 27:19

❖ *When Jesus spoke again to the people, he said, "I am the light of the world. Whoever follows me will never walk in darkness but will have the light of life."* John 8:12

❖ *Jesus said, "Believe in the light while you have the light, so that you may become children of light." John 12:36*

❖ *Jesus said, "In the same way, let your light shine before others, so that they may see your good deeds and glorify your Father in heaven."* Matthew 5:16

HYMNS FOR TODAY

Send the Light (Charles H. Gabriel, 1890)
Let Others See Jesus (B. B. McKinney)

Jesus, I must trust You as my Shepherd in these days of sadness and loneliness.

One day, I noticed a post that I had written earlier during the pandemic. My words were: I have done some weeping today. Sometimes, our circumstances can overcome us for a while. Seeing empty streets and empty grocery store shelves, sensing the loneliness of many people, and knowing that this is not normal is a gloomy picture. I hear God saying to me that it is okay to shed some tears because my heart is trusting in His grace and peace.

I felt safe and secure in our home with my husband. When I got out during those early days of the "stay at home" order, for essentials like going to the pharmacy or a medical appointment, my eyes would fill with tears and my throat would choke. Most businesses were closed. With the realization that adults and children were staying inside their homes, I noticed very little traffic and no school buses. So many jobs and education classes were only online. We had even been given a letter (if stopped) explaining that we had the right to drive to the Houston Methodist Hospital for Max's blood tests and treatments.

All these things saddened me, and I felt as if I was driving through a lonely valley. It was most important to trust in the "Good Shepherd," who is always with me to protect me and guide me as He fills me with His presence. Trusting in the goodness of God and continuing to praise Him for His peace was so much more comforting than being sad about things I did not understand or had no control over.

YOUR THOUGHTS

✓ Did you shed tears over situations during COVID? Or has there recently been another time of sadness for you where you shed some tears?

✓ How do you see Jesus as the Good Shepherd?

_____

_____

_____

_____

_____

_____

_____

_____

_____

GOD'S WORD

❖ *The LORD is my strength and my shield; my heart trusts in him, and he helps me. My heart leaps for joy, and with my song, I praise him.* Psalm 28:7

❖ *You will keep in perfect peace those whose minds are steadfast because they trust in you. Trust in the LORD forever, for the LORD, the LORD himself, is the eternal Rock.* Isaiah 26:3-4

❖ *"Though the mountains be shaken, and the hills be removed, yet my unfailing love for you will not be shaken, nor my covenant of peace be removed," says the LORD, who has compassion on you.* Isaiah 54:10

❖ *The LORD is my shepherd, I lack nothing. He makes me lie down in green pastures, he leads me beside quiet waters, he refreshes my soul. He guides me along the right paths for his name's sake. Even though I walk through the darkest valley, I will fear no evil for you are with me; your rod and your staff, they comfort me.* Psalm 23: 1-4

HYMNS FOR TODAY

The Lord's My Shepherd (Stuart Townend)

Gentle Shepherd (William and Gloria Gaither)

O, God in heaven, I desire to have a strong faith in You during these troubled times.

On a sunny Sunday morning in the summer, I found myself on the deck *under the shade tree*, basking in the day's beauty and giving thanks to God. Looking up into the sky, I noticed a jet streaming across the blue and then disappearing behind the clouds. I thought about the passengers on the airplane and the faith they must have to get on a jet and trust the pilot to get them to their destination. Furthermore, there was an overwhelming fear of contracting the virus during that specific time.

How were those passengers really feeling and thinking about being on an airplane? Did they feel safe and secure? Many people were not traveling at that time because there seemed to be so much anxiety about the safety of travel. How do people with problems and situations filled with confusion, worry, and anxiety endure? In life here on earth, we all can experience such issues from time to time and feel the need to trust in someone or something.

I thought about people really trusting each other. Are there some people we trust and others we do not trust? How do we trust the medical profession? How do we trust the safety of all areas of our lives? How do we trust the government, which seems to be so visible in our lives? I did *not* ponder that subject for very long because God reminded me that *my faith in Him gives me the ability to trust Him.*

So, my trust is in the one living God who loves and cares for all of us. My trust in God helps me in every situation, as well as the discernment to trust people here on earth as He leads me to do so. With that trust, I can make decisions that will help me through many issues these days.

These thoughts reminded me of a Sunday morning while teaching third-grade boys and girls. I taught them the acronym **F.A.I.T.H.** that I learned many years ago:

Forsaking **A**ll, **I** **T**rust **H**im. My faith comes from trusting in the one true, holy, and sovereign God.

YOUR THOUGHTS

✓ How do we discern God's thoughts and His will when we experience anxiety and confusion?

✓ How do we allow our faith to be strong during times of anxiety?

✓ How does the term "trust in God" relate to your daily life?

_____

_____

_____

_____

_____

_____

_____

_____

_____

_____

GOD'S WORD

❖ *But blessed is the one who trusts in the LORD, whose confidence is in him. They will be like a tree planted by water, that sends out its roots by the stream. It does not fear when heat comes; its leaves are always green. It has no worries in the year of drought and never fails to bear fruit. Jeremiah 17:7-8*

❖ *Trust in the LORD and do good; dwell in the land and enjoy safe pasture.* Psalm 37:3

❖ *Jesus said, "Do not let your hearts be troubled. You believe in God; believe also in me."* John 14:1

❖ *Now faith is confidence in what we hope for and assurance about what we do not see.* Hebrews 11:1

❖ *For in the gospel the righteousness of God is revealed, a righteousness that is by faith from first to last, just as it is written: "The righteous will live by faith."* Romans 1: 17

HYMNS FOR TODAY

Trusting Jesus (Edgar Page, 1876)

'Tis So Sweet to Trust in Jesus (Louisa M.R. Stead, 1882)

HONORING GOD

IN

PRAISING,

SHARING,

CELEBRATING,

AND LISTENING

> *God, I love You, and I praise You for the way*
> *You daily care for all the little things*
> *in my life.*

June 8th was another time for me to be in the car *under the shade tree* at Houston Methodist Hospital. My husband and I had chatted on the way to his 8:30 morning appointment about how God was still taking care of us. All his appointments for the summer months had been scheduled for 1:30 p.m. and 2:00 p.m.

During our phone conference with the hematologist in Houston the previous week, we were told that my husband needed to have early morning appointments for blood tests before taking medication. So, when I called the Infusion Center on Friday, the receptionist quickly changed all of them to morning times. The change made us happy as the afternoons were becoming unbearably hot in Texas.

Under the shade tree on that day, I read my Bible, spent time in prayer, listened to our choir music, and texted with Robert, my music and worship pastor. I also enjoyed a phone conversation with a friend and talked about how people are struggling with so many problems but that we must not allow ourselves to be overwhelmed by them. I told her about my firm belief in surrendering all my concerns to God and keeping them out of my mind. My thought is if I constantly dwell on them, I seem not to be trusting God. I most definitely believe that God's spiritual and physical healings are all in His timing.

Of course, Satan does not want God to be honored in this, so he tries to wear us down with worry, guilt, and doubts. We must keep "Praising God" every day for what He is doing. That day in June, we sang praises for a better appointment time and celebrated the news of my husband's improved blood count numbers.

YOUR THOUGHTS

✓ What are some specific ways that God took care of you during the pandemic or at a low time in your life?

✓ Are you praising God today for certain things he has done in your life?

_____

_____

_____

_____

_____

_____

_____

_____

_____

GOD'S WORD

❖ _He is the one you praise; he is your God, who performed for you those great and awesome wonders you saw with your own eyes._ Deuteronomy 10:21

❖ _My mouth is filled with your praise and declaring your splendor all day long._ Psalm 71:8

❖ _Sing to Him, sing praise to him; tell of all his wonderful acts._ I Chronicles 16:9

❖ _Blessed are those who dwell in your house; they are ever praising you._ Psalm 84:4

HYMNS FOR TODAY

 Let Us Just Praise the Lord (William and Gloria Gaither, 1972)

> *Lord, I am thankful for the life and liberties in my country, but I am most grateful for my freedom in Christ Jesus.*

July 4th was a day commemorating our country's independence from the rule of Great Britain in the year 1776. However, there were no big celebrations because of COVID. As I sat on our deck *under the shade tree* early that morning, my thoughts focused on the word freedom. For 244 years, our country has fought for and granted freedoms for our people.

Lately, there has been so much political unrest in our country, and *(in my opinion)* at times, there seems to be confusion about our government and freedoms and rights. Sometimes, there was the appearance of the good being punished and the wrong being glorified. Yes, it was bewildering and not as our founding fathers had planned.

I long for the time when people place greater emphasis on their freedom in Jesus Christ and the resulting joy and peace. His sacrificial death, burial, and resurrection freed us from being enslaved to a sinful nature. As believers in Jesus Christ, we enjoy the freedom to allow a living God to be in our lives and to bless us as we repent of our sinful nature and receive His grace and forgiveness. Max and I continued to be thankful for the liberties in our country, but were even more grateful for the truth and freedom given to us through the beautiful grace of Jesus Christ.

YOUR THOUGHTS

✓ What does freedom in Christ mean to you?

✓ What choices are we making in our lives that affect us as well as our families?

✓ Can some freedoms that we enjoy affect our spiritual life?

_____

_____

_____

_____

_____

_____

_____

_____

_____

GOD'S WORD

❖ *Jesus said, "So, if the Son sets you free, you will be free indeed."* John 8:36

❖ *It is for freedom that Christ has set us free. Stand firm, then and do not let yourselves be burdened again to a yoke of slavery.* Galatians 5:1

❖ *Now the Lord is the Spirit, and where the Spirit of the Lord is, there is freedom.* 2 Corinthians 3:17

❖ *Live as free people, but do not use your freedom as a cover-up for evil; but live as God's slaves.* I Peter 2:16

❖ *Jesus read, "The Spirit of the Lord is on me, because he has anointed me to proclaim good news to the poor. He has sent me to proclaim freedom to the prisoners and recovering of sight for the blind, to set the oppressed free, to proclaim the year of the Lord's favor."* Luke 4:18

HYMNS FOR TODAY

Wonderful Grace of Jesus (Haldor Lillenas, 1918)

Amazing Grace, My Chains are Gone (Chris Tomlin)

Father, I pray we humble ourselves, allowing the Holy Spirit to live and love through us so that others may know You.

With the pandemic and political unrest in our country, one could sense much hate and disagreements. One morning, while sitting on the deck *under the shade tree* and reading my Bible, I read about hate and then read many verses of love. Oh, how God wants us to love others! When a society of people is so self-centered and cares only about their own desires, how can that be love? As humans, our sense of hate or of love becomes an action towards others. As Christians following the teachings of Jesus, our hearts should be filled with love for others, even for our enemies and those with whom we might disagree.

My thoughts often return to an experience I had over forty years ago. I had the joy and privilege of serving in our church with teenagers in the mission organization called "Acteens." One weekend, we went to a conference at the University of Mary Hardin Baylor's campus.

During that conference, we heard a young missionary speak. She told how God had sent her to work in a village in a foreign country. Her assignment was to teach women to sew, cook, and teach them the Bible. One woman in the group was so loud and obnoxious that the missionary said, "I do not like her; I do not want her in this class, and I definitely cannot love her."

However, she felt God telling her to just be patient, pray for the woman, and let Him love through her. After a few weeks, the missionary noticed that the obnoxious lady was much calmer and happier and soon professed faith. The two also became good friends. The missionary's surrender to the Holy Spirit resulted in abundant fruit in her ministry, as she allowed God's love to flow through her actions every day.

Hopefully, all of us in attendance that day learned the importance of allowing God to love through us. What a different world this would be if we all loved God and let Him love through us!

YOUR THOUGHTS

✓ Are we aware of any hate, prejudices, or rebellion in our hearts?
✓ How do we, as Christians, fall short of demonstrating God's love to our world?

_____

_____

_____

_____

_____

_____

_____

_____

_____

_____

GOD'S WORD

❖ *Do not seek revenge or bear a grudge against anyone among your people, but love your neighbor as yourself, I am your LORD.* Leviticus 19:18

❖ *Ephesians 5:1 Walk the way of love, just as Christ loved us and gave himself up for us as a fragrant offering and sacrifice to God. Leviticus 19:18*

❖ *We love because He first loved us. Whoever claims to love God yet hates a brother or sister is a liar. For whoever does not love their brother or sister whom they have seen, cannot love God whom they have not seen.* I John 4:19-21

❖ *And now these three remain: faith, hope, and love. But the greatest of these is love.* I Corinthians 13:13

HYMNS FOR TODAY

 The Love of God (Federick M. Lehman, 1917)
Share His Love (William J. Reynolds, 1973)

Thank you, God, for those who continue to share Your love in service to others.

Dealing with health issues while being stuck at home was a completely new experience for my husband and me. Experiencing total isolation was difficult, but we adjusted well. We are blessed to have friends who, throughout those months, continued to keep us in their prayers. We received many uplifting cards from church friends and longtime friends. Neighbors offered to help us if we needed anything.

One day, my husband fell out on the driveway, and our neighbor Harold came quickly to help get him up. Our Life Group leaders left new Bible study books in our mailbox, and church staff members left lunch at our door. Friends mailed gift cards to local restaurants for us to use for takeout orders. Texts and phone calls were always a blessing. Even on the days when we did not get a card or a call, we knew friends were praying for us and would help us if we needed them. Yes, we were so grateful for our friends who so humbly and faithfully give and serve others. God's Spirit is so evident in their lives!

Another morning, while sitting *under the shade tree* at the medical center, I spent time in worship and prayer. I prayed that Max and I would make it home in time for our scheduled phone conference with another hematologist. As we finally arrived home and were walking through the front door, the phone rang.

Again, the timing was perfect. We had our phone conference, and then I drove to the local fast-food restaurant to get salads for lunch. Approaching the window to pay for our food, I was told that the car ahead of me had paid for my order. That had never happened to me before. I immediately thought about how I had seen God in so many things that morning, including a stranger serving a stranger.

By serving the Lord with gladness, Christians give honor to God. They are very much aware that their serving is through the power of the Holy Spirit.

YOUR THOUGHTS

✓ What do you think are the essential characteristics of people who serve God?
✓ What are some specific ways you have seen God serve you through others?

_____

_____

_____

_____

_____

_____

_____

_____

_____

_____

GOD'S WORD

❖ *God has shown you, O mortal, what is good. And what does the LORD require of you? To act justly, and to love mercy, and to walk humbly with your God.* Micah 6:8

❖ *You, brothers and sisters, were called to be free. But do not use your freedom to indulge the flesh; rather, serve one another humbly in love. For the entire law is fulfilled in keeping this one command: Love your neighbor as yourself.* Galatians 5:13-14

❖ *For what we preach is not ourselves, but Jesus Christ as Lord and ourselves as your servants for Jesus' sake.* 2 Corinthians 4:5

HYMNS FOR TODAY

 The Longer I Serve Him (William and Gloria Gaither)

God, I am so grateful that our Christian foundation is on the Solid Rock of Jesus.

Playing and singing hymns at my piano often brought back memories of my childhood and teenage years. It seemed as if each one had a remarkable memory and a heart-warming message. On July 18, 2020, our son drove us to visit with Celeste, and we sat in her front yard. When staying with her, we always heard lots of stories, and she had many because she was almost 101 years of age. Many of the stories she and my husband shared were about life in a small town where their lives seemed to be centered on school and church. They enjoyed living in a time when life seemed full of love and respect for each other and cherished many fun memories.

My husband and I were blessed with a firm foundation rooted in the Word of God, the resurrected Savior, and an abundant life with the Holy Spirit. This foundation was filled with memories of seeing God in many faithful people through the years and the power of their individual testimonies for their Lord. These were people whose lives had had many heartaches, sufferings, and losses, yet were so dedicated to trusting and following Jesus. Their lives were built on the foundation of Jesus Christ, their solid rock.

Max and I would often talk about people in our past who had been such a strong spiritual influence on our lives. One such man was Mr. Green, who was the Bible teacher for our young couples' Sunday morning class during our early years of marriage. Mr. Green knew how to minister to us on Sunday mornings and during the week. He was a man with a kind and gentle spirit, who was so dedicated to loving and serving his Lord and Savior. God used him in the Spiritual growth of many in our group, especially the men.

I am convinced that our solid Christian foundation gave us days of joy and peace during the pandemic and coping with my husband's illnesses. Biblical truths and godly people throughout our lives were a big part of God's blessings that indeed helped sustain our faith during that challenging time.

YOUR THOUGHTS

✓ What do you consider the foundation of your faith?

✓ Name ways that your Christian foundation has helped you during difficult times in life.

_____

_____

_____

_____

_____

_____

_____

_____

_____

_____

GOD'S WORD

❖ *I have hidden Your word in my heart so that I might not sin against You.* Psalm 119:11

❖ *You shall love the Lord you God with all your heart and all your soul and with all your strength and with all your mind, and your neighbor as yourself.* Luke 10:27

❖ *Do your best to present yourself to God as one approved, a worker who does not need to be ashamed and who correctly handles the word of truth.* 2 Timothy 2:15

❖ *Jesus said, "Therefore, everyone who hears these words of mine and puts them into practice is like a wise man who built his house upon the rock. The rain came down, the streams rose, and winds blew and beat against the house, yet it did not fall because it had its foundation on the rock."* Matthew 7:24-25

HYMNS FOR TODAY

 The Solid Rock (Edward Mote, 1834)

> *Thank You, Lord, for the blessings of Your presence and Your faithfulness to us.*

During the last week in July 2020, Max and I experienced an unexpected nighttime trip to the hospital. Our son had spent the evening with us, enjoying a meal and watching some old Western shows before returning home. My husband was having some problems relating to his bladder cancer, and on that Wednesday night, he was suffering from extreme pain.

Around 10:00 p.m. he asked me to drive him to the Emergency Room. I had to bring him to Houston Methodist in The Woodlands because they had his complete medical records. As we traveled from our home on the lake, I noticed traffic was heavy for nighttime. My husband was in so much pain that he could not really carry on a conversation. I just kept driving and praying, knowing that God was with us and would get us safely to our destination.

A comforting thought came to me—one that so many of our friends often shared with us: "I pray for you every night." So, I just kept that in my thoughts. Our son met us there, and we could not go into the hospital because of the COVID restrictions. So, we sat in the parking lot, texting and talking with our daughter in California. I just kept praying that my husband could go home with me. And I was so grateful that I was not alone in the parking lot at night.

Thankfully, my husband finally called for me to pick him up, and we got home after 2:00 a.m. He came home feeling better but with a catheter. We were so thankful for prayers and God's answering the prayer that he would not be kept in the hospital since restrictions would not allow us to visit him. I had secretly laughed all the way home because as I drove, my husband was giving me driving instructions, just as he would have done with one of his teenage students. It was a little annoying, but I was so happy to be driving him home, so I just kept smiling. I think God knew I needed some "humor" on that night.

The unexpected circumstances of that night blessed me with seeing God answer several prayers. I felt secure in His presence during those hours. God again showed us His faithfulness.

YOUR THOUGHTS

✓ Have you ever felt God's presence and knew your friends were praying for you?
✓ Has unexpected humor ever helped you through a tough time?

_____

_____

_____

_____

_____

_____

_____

_____

_____

_____

GOD'S WORD

❖ *Be strong and courageous, do not be afraid or terrified, for the LORD your God goes with you, He will never leave you nor forsake you.* Deuteronomy 31:6

❖ *Then you will call on me and come and pray to me, and I will listen to you.* Jeremiah 29:12

❖ *Blessed are those who have learned to acclaim you, who walk in the light of your presence, Lord.* Psalm 89:15

❖ *And so, from the day we heard, we have not ceased to pray for you, asking that you may be filled with the knowledge of his will in all spiritual wisdom and understanding.* Colossians 1:9

❖ *Rejoice always, pray without ceasing, give thanks in all circumstances, for this is the will of God in Christ Jesus for you.* I Thessalonians 5:16-18

HYMNS FOR TODAY

 In His Presence (Dick and Mel Tunney, 1989)

God, I see a cloudy day in the weather, and I feel a stormy day in our lives. I honor Your faithfulness in calming our days.

On a cloudy Friday morning (following the trip to the ER), I took my husband to see his urologist. While sitting in the car, the doctor called to inform me of the need to do another TURBT surgical procedure. And he wanted to do it the following Friday (August 7). But we would celebrate our fiftieth wedding anniversary on that day. The doctor was so thoughtful and scheduled it for Monday, August 3rd, instead.

I drove to the entrance of the building and found my husband still with the catheter as he came out. My heart ached for him for his discomfort. We went to another building for blood tests and a COVID test, all to prepare for the procedure on Monday. Finally, we drove home and had lunch. We were relaxing and getting some rest from the busy morning. Then we received a call to return to the Houston Methodist Infusion Center for another blood test. So, we had another drive in Friday afternoon traffic.

Once again, as I sat in the car *under the shade tree*, thoughts about this storm overwhelmed me. The Holy Spirit quickly reminded me of Jesus' power as He walked the sea and calmed the storm. Through this demonstration, his disciples learned his true identity and power.

There seemed to be so many twists and turns in our lives during those days. Nonetheless, my husband and I understood the importance of relying on God each day for a peaceful, calm spirit, having unwavering faith in His plan, and expressing gratitude daily. He was walking through this storm with us. Yes, throughout the stormy days, we still had many blessings given to us by our Heavenly Father. We often would say: "It is with faith in God that we walk through these days, and as they pass, we always see God's hand in it all."

YOUR THOUGHTS

✓ What are some ways you see God calming your stormy days?
✓ What have you learned about yourself and God in the twists and turns of life?

_____

_____

_____

_____

_____

_____

_____

_____

_____

GOD'S WORD

❖ *Then he got into the boat and his disciples followed him. Suddenly a furious storm came up on the lake, so the waves swept over the boat. But Jesus was sleeping. The disciples went and woke him, saying, "Lord, save us! We are going to drown!" He replied, "You of little faith, why are you so afraid?" Then he got up and rebuked the winds and the waves, and it was completely calm. The men were amazed and asked," What at kind of man is this? Even the winds and the waves obey him!"* Matthew 8:23-27

❖ *Even to your old age and gray hairs, I am He, I am He who will sustain you.* Isaiah 46:4

❖ *Now may the Lord of peace himself give you peace at all times in every way. The Lord be with all of you.* 2 Thessalonians 3:16

❖ *Many, LORD my God, are the wonders you have done, the things you have planned for us. None can compare with you; were I to speak and tell of your deeds, they would be too many to declare.* Psalm 40:5

HYMNS FOR TODAY

 When the Storms of Life Are Raging, Stand by Me
(Charles A. Tindley, 1905)

God, today is another day of ups and downs.
My mind asks questions, but I know You are
my powerful living God.

The Monday of the surgery came quickly. And I found myself parked *under the shade tree* once again. My husband was scheduled for blood transfusions and the surgical procedure. He soon called to say that he would receive two units of blood and be there for at least four hours. After that, I would need to pick him up to drive him to the door of the hospital where the surgery was scheduled.

With a bit of time to spare, I decided to make a quick trip to Walmart for a bathroom break and to grab a few items we needed. Returning to the hospital to find a shade tree, I then sat in my car waiting for Max's call. At 11:30 a.m., someone in surgery called asking about my husband. He was still at the Infusion Center, so they sent someone over to take him in a wheelchair from Building One to the hospital.

My time was spent praying for the surgical procedure. I talked with a friend on the phone who prayed with me. Our son arrived with lunch, and we spent the next few hours together waiting for Max to be dismissed.

On that day, we happened to park closer to the interstate feeder road, and the noise level was quite a distraction. These noises made me wonder, "Why is this pandemic still going on?" For that matter, why are people suffering? Does God have a purpose in this? Do I have the right to ask my HOLY GOD these questions?

I am someone who wants to know answers like everyone else. How can I have doubts and questions if I trust in Jesus and live daily with the Holy Spirit in my life?

Yes, I soon realized that my focus in life should not be on those questions and concerns. My focus should be on worshipping God, living life as a believer in Jesus Christ, and hoping for Jesus' return one day to take us to heaven as He has promised.

YOUR THOUGHTS

✓ What are some of your concerns and questions about the hard days of life?

✓ How do you think God wants us to live in these times?

_____

_____

_____

_____

_____

_____

_____

_____

_____

_____

GOD'S WORD

❖ *Call on me in the day of trouble; I will deliver you, and you will honor me.*
Psalm 50:15

❖ *For the grace of God has appeared that offers salvation to all people. It teaches us to say "no" to ungodliness and worldly passions, and to live self-controlled, upright and godly lives in this present age, while we wait for blessed hope-the appearing of the glory of our great God and Savior, Jesus Christ, who gave himself for us to redeem us from all wickedness and to purify for himself a people that are his very own eager to do what is good. Titus 2:11-14*

❖ *Jesus said, "Do not let your hearts be troubled. You believe in God; believe also in me. My Father's house has many rooms; if that were not so, would I have told you that I going to prepare a place for you? And if I go and prepare a place for you, I will come back and take you to be with me that you also may be where I am."* John 14: 1-3

HYMNS FOR TODAY

Be Thou My Vision (Ancient Irish, Mary Byrne)
We Shall Behold Him (Dottie Rambo, 1980)

> *We honor You, God, on this day as we the happiness and blessings of our fifty years of marriage.*

My husband and I always woke up early, and our greeting for each other was always, "I love you!" On the first Friday in August 2020, we celebrated our 50th wedding anniversary with hearts overflowing with thanksgiving to God. For a few months, I had wondered how or if we would celebrate. But what a fantastic day we had!

God blessed us with family and friends who love us. We felt thankful to have our son by our side that day. He came with a decorated cake, ginger ale for toast, and a huge banner to display. On the dining table, he arranged a laptop connected to a large-screen television, and we shared a Zoom time with some of our long-time closest friends. Later, our son prepared us a wonderful steak dinner served on our original wedding dishes.

In the evening, we had another Zoom anniversary "party" with family from all over Texas and California joining us. It was so wonderful to see their faces and converse with them. They were all so gracious to us in sharing their congratulations, and they gave us such kind greetings and cherished memories. They even played a slide show of photos from our wedding and family over the years. The background music was "The Wedding Prayer," a song that was sung at our wedding on August 7, 1970, at First Baptist Church in Plano, Texas.

Many asked what had kept us together for fifty years. Max and I quickly acknowledged that the key to our marriage was our relationship with God, which fosters daily love and respect for each other. We had seen God's blessings in all our days, even during times of failing health or disappointments with situations of life.

The party was so fun, and we loved every minute. We also appreciated all who called us, sent cards, and took part in the Zoom event.

Just a couple of months before, the doctors had told us that my husband probably had six months to live. However, we never focused on that or talked about it. We just continued to live, following the doctor's orders, and trusting in God and enjoying our days. Our fiftieth wedding anniversary was a special occasion to rejoice in the blessings God has given our marriage. We were so thankful for our years together, as well as for the family and friends who have shared a life with us.

YOUR THOUGHTS

✓ Did you have a special celebration or a lifetime event during the pandemic?
✓ How did you celebrate?
✓ How did you see God's blessings in that event?

GOD'S WORD

❖ *Enter his gates with thanksgiving and his courts with praise; give thanks to him and praise his name. For the LORD is good and his love endures forever; his faithfulness continues through all generations.* Psalm 100:4-5

❖ *But at the beginning of creation God made them male and female. For this reason a man will leave his father and mother and be united to his wife, and the two will become one flesh.* Mark 10:6-8

❖ *Be devoted to one another in love. Honor one another above yourselves.* Romans 12:10

❖ *Husbands, love your wives just as Christ loved the church and gave himself up for her.* Ephesians 5:25

❖ *However, each one of you must love his wife as he loves himself; and the wife must respect her husband.* Ephesians 5:33

HYMNS FOR TODAY

 O Perfect Love (Dorothy Gurney, 1883)
The Wedding Prayer (Wesley Putnam)

The last week of August 2020 was quite a rollercoaster. We were waiting for the results of the bone marrow biopsy. Family and friends were calling about it. Finally, on Tuesday morning, we got a call to meet with the hematologist in The Woodlands at 10:00. I was so grateful that I could go in with my husband to see the hematologist. She related to us that Max's bone marrow was worse. Since the pills weren't effective, she removed him from all medication. She also told us that a chemotherapy treatment approved for his disease would be the next step, so we left the office with that plan.

On Wednesday morning, we received a message on the medical chart that Max was scheduled for another bone marrow biopsy on September 1st at the Houston Methodist Outpatient Center in downtown Houston. We were not expecting that! It was over an hour away, so I called to inquire.

Therefore, this was the new plan agreed upon by both his hematologists before any treatments. Our son had gone out of state, so I would be alone in taking Max to downtown Houston. I started researching travel options to Houston, which was overwhelming, as I had never driven there before. However, through prayer, God assured me, "I will help you."

On Friday, I called to ask questions about the appointment. To my surprise, the lady told me I could go to the hospital with my husband. That was a "Praise God" moment for me, and I excitedly called my friend, Sue, to give her the good news.

After the call, I thanked God once more because Sue and Andy promised to give us a ride to Houston. What a relief and a blessing! Once again, I experienced the blessing of waiting on God and trusting His promise of presence and provision.

On August 31, as I sat *under the shade tree* again, waiting for my husband to have another blood transfusion, I received a call from Sue. She mentioned that Andy needed an appointment downtown on the same day, as they would take Max and me for his treatment. So she had called earlier that day to obtain one and was given an appointment at 2:00 p.m., the same time as our appointment! That was no coincidence; we both agreed it was God's plan. He is so faithful to take care of all the details of our needs.

YOUR THOUGHTS

✓ Name a time when you honestly had to allow God to take care of a situation.
✓ Tell about a time when you saw God take care of your needs when others might call it a coincidence.

_____

_____

_____

_____

_____

_____

_____

_____

_____

_____

GOD'S WORD

❖ *I remain confident of this: I will seek the goodness of the LORD in the land of the living. Wait for the LORD; be strong and take heart and wait for the LORD.* Psalm 27:13-14

❖ *We wait in hope for the LORD; he is our help and our shield.* Psalm 33:20

❖ *Yet the LORD longs to be gracious to you; therefore, he will rise up to show you compassion. For the LORD is a God of justice. Blessed are all who wait for Him.* Isaiah 30:18

HYMNS FOR TODAY

 He's Been Faithful (Carol Cymbala)

God, I am so grateful that I can listen for Your voice in the midst of life's circumstances.

One beautiful fall afternoon, I was enjoying a cool breeze while sitting on our deck *under the shade tree.* I noticed several sounds: the sounds of a riding lawn mower next door, the noise from a low-flying airplane, and the voices of people as they walked on the path behind our house. Max and I were grateful for our home and the sweet sounds of our neighborhood. On that Sunday, we enjoyed being with Life Groups on Zoom for Bible study and joined in on our church's live-streamed worship service. We felt blessed to hear God's voice while participating in those opportunities provided by our church through the Internet.

I began thinking that even with the loud noises surrounding me, I could "be quiet, call His name, and listen to God" while sitting on the deck. It is so important to let go of all the things cluttering my thoughts that keep me from knowing more about God and listening to Him.

It was such a pleasure listening to God again through the music the birds were providing! God spoke to me in my observation of His care of a bird enjoying the bird bath. God communicated with me while I was seeking forgiveness for the times I had failed my Lord. I sensed God helping me with my confusing thoughts about the unusual happenings of life.

It was a blessing to have peace while hearing God speak through my thoughts, focusing on His faithfulness over the past week. I continued to praise God for all He had given to us in the challenging days of life and for His constant speaking to us in various ways through the power of the Holy Spirit.

YOUR THOUGHTS

- ✓ How can we have a quiet time and know God when surrounded by the noises of the world?
- ✓ How do we hear God's voice?
- ✓ What are some blessings you experienced recently or during the noisy times of life?

_____

_____

_____

_____

_____

_____

_____

_____

_____

_____

GOD'S WORD

- ❖ *He says, "Be still and know that I am God; I will be exalted among the nations. I will be exalted in the earth." Psalm 46:10*

- ❖ *I will listen to what God the LORD says; he promises peace to his people, his faithful servants. Psalm 85:8*

- ❖ *Whether you turn to the right or to the left, your ears will hear a voice behind you saying, "This is the way, walk in it." Isaiah 30:21*

❖ *Jesus said, "My sheep listen to my voice; I know them, and they follow me."* John 10:27

❖ *For the eyes of the Lord are on the righteous and his ears are attentive to his prayer, but the face of the Lord is against those who do evil.* I Peter 3:12

HYMNS FOR TODAY

 Speak to My Heart (B. B. McKinney)

BEING ANCHORED IN GOD'S LOVE, GRACE, PEACE AND HOPE

Dear God, as I enter your throne room today,
I desire to see You in all things, especially in
our weaknesses and our souls' heartaches.

I chauffeured my husband to his appointments on September 14, 2020, and left him at the entrance. However, I did not sit *under a shade tree* that day, but quickly parked the car and rushed in behind him because he was so weak and dehydrated. There was a strict check-in process with COVID questions, using hand sanitizer, and checking my temperature. The Infusion Center receptionist allowed me to sit in the waiting room (if I wore my mask) since no one else was there.

My husband had such difficulty walking after the blood testing procedure that the nurse had to bring him a wheelchair. She took him to the hematologist's office, and we met with the doctor. Her eyes revealed sadness as she explained that chemotherapy was not an option because of his weak body. The next thing for him to do was to be in hospice care at home.

This kind doctor had spent a year and a half helping Max with his blood disease. She requested to talk with our son, so I called and put him on the speakerphone. Then, they took my husband back to the Infusion Center for blood transfusion and IV fluids. They dismissed us and allowed us to go home after we had been there for five hours.

The treatments Max got that day gave him strength, while I relied on God for the strength to drive us home and be ready for the last days with my husband. As I drove off the parking lot, my heart was so full of gratitude for the *shade trees* that had been my sanctuary there for many months. I was so glad to be taking my husband home with me!

Although we didn't get the news we wanted, we had faith that God was taking care of us. More than ever, I knew we would need to lean on God for our journey of the uncertain days ahead. I also knew that my husband's strong faith in His Lord would continue to help me endure, as we both trusted in God's grace to supply our needs.

YOUR THOUGHTS

✓ How has God helped you through a time of receiving extremely sad news?
✓ As you look back at some tragic times, what are some things for which you can thank God?

_____

_____

_____

_____

_____

_____

_____

_____

_____

_____

GOD'S WORD

❖ *Humble yourselves, therefore, under God's mighty hand, that he may lift you up in due time. Cast all your anxieties on him because he cares for you.* I Peter 5:6-7

❖ *Surely the righteous will never be shaken; they will be remembered forever. They will have no fear of bad news; their hearts are steadfast, trusting in the LORD.* Psalm 112:6-7

❖ *I can do all this through him who gives me strength.* Philippians 4:13

HYMNS FOR TODAY

 Leaning on the Everlasting Arms (E A. Hoffman, 1887)
It is Well with My Soul (Horatio G. Spafford, 1873)

O, God, my heart is full of gratitude for the compassion that flows through others to help us in our time of need.

Our last day at Houston Methodist was sad for us even as we continued to see such incredible love and care. For months during the pandemic, I had not been able to accompany my husband for his blood work and transfusions. But on that day, I could sit in the waiting room of the Infusion Center. However, if a patient came in, I would need to leave the room.

The news we were given about hospice care evoked a lot of emotions in me. Soon, two of the nurses (familiar faces) came out to me and told me they wanted me to be with my husband—but they would take me in a back way. So, we went out to the lobby and down some empty hallways, and then I was in a room with Max. The moment I walked into the room, his face lit up with a big smile.

We were there for three hours or more. A nurse gave me a warm blanket because it was cold in the room. Their generosity in letting us have that time together was greatly appreciated. The nurses were always so sweet and kind to Max every time he went into the Infusion Center for over eighteen months. They always talked and laughed with him and even had a nickname for him. He always felt comfortable with them.

How grateful we are for dedicated medical teams who love and care for people in such a critical time of their lives. We always sensed that the presence of our loving God was flowing through them. Such kindness and compassion must be the work of our Holy God!

YOUR THOUGHTS

✓ Write about a time when someone was incredibly kind to you?

✓ What are situations where we can show compassion and kindness to others?

_____

_____

_____

_____

_____

_____

_____

_____

_____

GOD'S WORD

❖ *Whoever is kind to the poor lends to the LORD, and he will reward them for what they have done.* Proverbs 19:17

❖ *May the God who gives endurance and encouragement give you the same attitude of mind toward each other that Jesus Christ had, so with one mind and one voice you may glorify the God and Father of our Lord Jesus Christ.* Romans 15:5

❖ *Finally, all of you, be like-minded, be sympathetic, love one another, be compassionate and humble.* 1 Peter 3:8

HYMNS FOR TODAY

 The Servant Song (Richard Gillard, 1977)

God, I am grateful for Your care of our emotional needs as You guide our steps with Your peace.

The first hospice visit was scheduled for September 15, 2020. I sensed my husband's anxiety about the idea of hospice and strangers coming into our home. Both of us prayed for God to provide what he needed for that visit.

So, on the first day of hospice care, nurse Karen came in and spent time getting to know us. Max told her that he had been a high school coach. I chimed in to say to her that he had coached high school students for thirty-seven years, and he had even played college football. She asked him, "What college?"

He told her he had played at the University of Arizona. She immediately said to us that she was from Arizona and had also gone to UA. From that point on, their connection solidified, making it effortless for Max to feel comfortable and communicate with her. I saw it as another way; God was taking care of him and providing for his need to feel relaxed with a stranger.

During that first hospice meeting, we were unclear on some decisions, so Karen suggested that she return later in the week when our son could join us in the decisions. We had a follow-up meeting and made decisions about how to care for Max. Every time Karen visited, we shared conversation and laughter. She took the time to truly understand us, including our faith in God, our love story, our long-time marriage, and everything about our family. She was great at ordering all the supplies that were needed for the next few weeks.

My husband was grateful that he and Karen focused on the fun times of life and laughing together. I witnessed moments of peace in my husband's life when the nurses arrived. Again, I was praising God for His presence, especially during times of nurses in our home.

YOUR THOUGHTS

✓ Tell about an experience where you saw God open the door to a relationship that really helped you.

✓ How have you seen God give you peace in an uncertain situation?

_____

_____

_____

_____

_____

_____

_____

_____

_____

_____

GOD'S WORD

❖ *But when you pray, go into your room, close the door, and pray to your Father who is unseen. Then your Father who sees what is done in secret, will reward you.* Matthew 6:6

❖ *Therefore since we have been justified through faith, we have peace with God through our Lord Jesus Christ, through who we have gained access by faith into this grace in which we now stand. And we boast in the hope of the glory of God.* Romans 5:1-2

❖ *But, you dear friends, by building yourself up in your most holy faith and praying in the Holy Spirit, keep yourselves in God's love as you wait for the mercy of our Lord Jesus Christ to bring you to eternal life.* Jude 1:20-21

HYMNS FOR TODAY

 Where the Spirit of the Lord Is (Stephen R. Adams, 1973)

> *Dear Lord, thank You for the anchor of love*
> *for family.*

During the weeks as my husband and I were entering the time of his hospice care, we were privileged to have family members visit. They came at different times so we could focus on who was here and really spend time with each of them. My two sisters and their spouses came for visits. Max's sister and her husband came from California in their motor home. We really enjoyed spending time with all of them.

Our daughter and three grandchildren flew in from California for a long weekend visit. I even prepared a Thanksgiving Dinner for us to enjoy as we thanked God for the blessings of our lives in the good times and the difficult times. For several months, our home had had no family except for our son, who faithfully came to be with us.

What a joy it is to talk, laugh, reminisce, and share time with one another! None of our families are perfect, but being in one is such a blessing. Our love for family members must be "unconditional," as Christ loved us unconditionally and gave Himself for us. There is such comfort in knowing the love of family and the feeling of belonging.

Late one day in the cool of the evening, as I sat *under the shade tree* in our backyard, I thought about each person in my family and prayed for them. I thank God for them. I thought about the "wonder" and the "miracle" of God's great love for each of us, and I saw that love is the beautiful, strong foundation of the family unit.

YOUR THOUGHTS

✓ Reflect on a time when being with family was very important to you.

✓ What is unique about unconditional love in a family?

_____

_____

_____

_____

_____

_____

_____

_____

_____

_____

_____

GOD'S WORD

❖ *Children are a heritage from the LORD, offspring a reward from him.* Psalm 127:3

❖ *Children's children are a crown to the aged, and parents are the pride of their children.* Proverbs 17:6

❖ *We love because he first loved us.* 1 John 4:19

❖ *Fathers, do not exasperate your children; instead, bring them up in the training and instruction of the Lord.* Ephesians 6:4

❖ *How good and pleasant it is when God's people live together in unity!* Psalm 133:1

❖ *Bear with each other and forgive one another if any of you has a grievance against someone. Forgive as the Lord forgave you. And over all these virtues put on love, which binds them all together in perfect unity.* Colossians 3:13-14

HYMNS FOR TODAY

The Wonder of It All (George Beverly Shea, 1956)

Think About His Love (Walt Harrah, 1987)

> *God, I am so grateful for beautiful surprises that bless and enrich our lives.*

One gorgeous fall morning, I awoke as always, talking and listening to God. I went through my routine of helping my husband get dressed, enjoying breakfast together, and hooking up oxygen for him. We continued to be content and at peace with our lives. I finished doing laundry and prepared a list of essential things that need to be done. We watched a Bible teaching, then spent some time talking. Later, I went out on the deck to visit with our son. There was a noise at the front of the house, so I went to the front window and saw a white vehicle parked in front of our home.

The phone rang shortly, and our friends Will and Vicki called to inform us they left a gift at our doorstep. Well, I immediately invited them in for a visit; it was so good to see them. The visit was unexpected, and the gift of a stained-glass piece that Vicki had crafted for us was indeed a beautiful surprise. What a blessing their visit was to us that day!

We enjoyed the talk and laughter so much and appreciated Will voicing a prayer for us before they left. It was beautiful to experience so much Christian love during this visit. That night before bed, Max talked about how much fun he had had with our friends. It was perfect to get to know Vicki with her stories and laughter, which we don't see on Sunday mornings in our Life Group.

Our loving God knew how much Max and I both needed such a visit on that day, mainly because we had been isolated and hadn't received any guests in our home for a while. What a blessing!

YOUR THOUGHTS

✓ Tell about a time when someone surprised you with goodness, and you knew it was of God.

✓ How did you respond to that surprise?

_____

_____

_____

_____

_____

_____

_____

_____

_____

_____

GOD'S WORD

❖ *Therefore, as we have opportunity, let us do good to all people, especially to those who belong to the family of believers.* Galatians 6:10

❖ *Share with the Lord's people who are in need. Practice hospitality.* Romans 12:13

❖ *Jesus said, "A new command I give you: Love one another. As I have loved you, so you must love one another. By this, everyone will know that you are my disciples if you love one another."* John 13:34-35

❖ *I pray that your partnership with us in the faith may be effective in deepening your understanding of every good thing that we share for the sake of Christ. Your love has given me great joy and encouragement because you have refreshed the hearts of the Lord's people.* Philemon 1:6-7

HYMNS FOR TODAY

 Make Me a Blessing (Ira B. Wilson, 1909)

Lord, You are our anchor and our strength for the days and nights when we are physically weak.

The past few days had been so difficult seeing my husband go through a new stage of his disease. My heart ached as I saw him getting weaker. Yet, in that physical weakness, I knew Max continued to be anchored with a strong faith in His Lord. Our faith provided us with the strength to reach out to our loved ones. God gave us the mental strength to make decisions while lovingly encouraging each other.

My husband continued to live with a positive attitude. He looked forward to spending time with our son and others who came to visit. He enjoyed conversation and laughter with the nurses who came into our home; he appreciated their care. I continued to be so very grateful that Max's calm, easy-going personality remained the same throughout the days of pain and weakness.

Our love for each other had always been anchored in our loving God, especially during the stormy days of life. We were now experiencing a *new* storm. Praise God, we were secure in His loving care that provided all our needs, including giving Max the mental and physical strength to visit with family and friends, which was so vital to us at this time.

YOUR THOUGHTS

✓ What are physical strength and mental strength?
✓ Tell about a time when you were weak and felt God provide the strength you needed.

_____

_____

_____

_____

_____

_____

_____

_____

_____

GOD'S WORD

❖ *The Lord is my strength and my defense; he has become my salvation. He is my God, and I will praise him, my father's God, and I will exalt him.* Exodus 15:2

❖ *He gives strength to the weary and increases the power of the weak.* Isaiah 40:29

❖ *And the God of all grace, who called you to His eternal glory in Christ, after you have suffered a little while, will himself restore you, and make you strong and steadfast.* I Peter 5:10

❖ *My flesh and my heart may fail, but God is the strength of my heart and my portion forever.* Psalm 73:26

❖ *We have this hope as an anchor for the soul, firm and secure.* Hebrews 6:19

HYMNS FOR TODAY

The Anchor Holds (Lawrence Chewning, 1992)
In Times Like These (Ruth Caye Jones, 1944)

Thank you, Heavenly Father, for Your calm assurance in my heart and Your guidance filled with wisdom.

On October 5th I decided it was time to go to the funeral home again. So I made an appointment with Heather, the funeral director. She was so kind and helpful and totally understanding of my heart. When I returned home, it was a delight to see my husband talking and laughing with some of his college friends who wanted to spend some time with him. I also received a call from one of our ministers with encouraging words.

Later, I was looking again at the hospice care booklet and realized that the hospice nurse would call the funeral home when the time came, which was comforting to know. So, I was highly grateful to God's leadership in making that visit with Heather to resume the process of my final acts of love for my beloved husband. My family was so very appreciative of the compassionate hospice team and funeral home staff.

During that time, I felt God guiding me in many small moments, helping me make decisions and navigate unfamiliar situations. Being in tune with the guidance of the Holy Spirit always gives me the wisdom that I need, as well as incredible calm in stormy situations. And that is how I lived those days. Only a loving God could give us so much peace during our last days together on this earth!

YOUR THOUGHTS

✓ Have you seen God's guidance in recent days or at a critical time in your life?
✓ Can your acknowledgment of His peace and guidance be a witness to others?

_____

_____

_____

_____

_____

_____

_____

_____

_____

_____

GOD'S WORD

❖ *Cast all your anxiety on him because he cares for you.* I Peter 5:7

❖ *If any of you lacks wisdom, you should ask God, who gives generously to all without finding fault, and it will be given to you.* James 1:5

❖ *Have I not commanded you? Be strong and courageous. Do not be afraid, do not be discouraged for the LORD your God will be with you wherever you go.* Joshua 1:9

❖ *Jesus said, "I have told you these things so that in me you may have peace. In this world, you will have trouble. But take heart! I have overcome the world."* John 16:33

HYMNS FOR TODAY

 Peace, Wonderful Peace (W. D. Cornell)

> *God, I thank You for our pastor, who loves*
> *and cares for his congregation.*

Throughout my husband's lengthy illness, our pastor frequently reached out via phone or text. The church staff often prayed for us, and many of them would email, call, or text frequently. The year prior to my husband going into hospice, we spent a week with our pastor, his wife, and a group from our church at Glen Eyrie in Colorado Springs for a beautiful retreat. We even celebrated my husband's birthday while there.

During hospice care, our pastor came to visit with us. My husband shared with him about when he made his profession of faith as a child and his favorite Bible verse. We continued to be so thankful that our pastor knows us personally and isn't someone we only see in the pulpit on Sunday mornings.

Pastor Jeff assured us that the church would provide a memorial service in our sanctuary and have it live-streamed. He would also lead a graveside service with us before the memorial service. We were really content with that plan, especially considering that many family and friends wouldn't be able to make it. We both had peace in our hearts as we saw God continuing to take care of us at this very critical time in our lives.

None of us ever fully appreciate or understand the dedication of a pastor who gives so much to his congregation—especially during the loss of a loved one. It is the family's enormous loss, but also a loss to the pastor who has ministered to a member of his congregation. I am so grateful for Pastor Jeff, who humbly loves and serves God's people. It must be the *deep love of our Heavenly Father* that enables him to preach the Word, as well as minister to us, in times of great loss.

YOUR THOUGHTS

✓ Do you have a relationship with your pastor?
✓ Write about a time(s) when ministers have helped you?

_____

_____

_____

_____

_____

_____

_____

_____

_____

_____

GOD'S WORD

❖ *Be shepherds of God's flock that is under your care, watching over them, not because you must, but because you are willing, as God wants you to be; not pursuing dishonest gain, but eager to serve.* I Peter 5:2

❖ *Keep watch over yourselves and to all the flock by which the Holy Spirit has made you overseers.* Acts 20:28

❖ *Preach the word, be prepared in season and out of season; correct, rebuke, and encourage, with great patience and careful instruction.* 2 Timothy 4:2

❖ *But God demonstrates his own love for us in this: While we were still sinners, Christ died for us.* Romans 5:8

HYMNS FOR TODAY

 How Deep the Father's Love for Us (Stuart Townend, 1995)

Dear God, I continually praise You with my lips for Your goodness to us in these days.

During the final days of hospice care, along with our son, family members took turns coming for a visit. One day, Max's college friends (football teammates) called to inquire about coming. His roommate, Royce, came one day, and we had such a good visit. Another day, Leroy and Leon came, and it was such an enjoyable visit for all these longtime friends.

It was nice to have conversations and laughter with friends at our home. Our friends Pat and Bobby came a couple of times, and we enjoyed old stories of their coaching years and fishing tournaments together. Phone calls from other coaches my husband had worked with over the years were enjoyable for him.

Our longtime friends, Linda, Maxie, and Holly came and spent Max's last Sunday afternoon with us. We thoroughly enjoyed talking about our almost fifty years of friendship and recalling great memories. It was indeed a blessed Sunday! The following Tuesday, another friend wanted to come. As Max's health declined, we realized that he could no longer receive visitors.

But God blessed my husband with the right ones to spend time with during those last days. I hold dear the photos and a small video capturing some of the visits. Max was happy and enjoyed reminiscing with family and friends. Often at night, when we went to bed, he told me how much he enjoyed the visits. He talked about the kindness and compassion of those faithful ones in our lives. We both knew how blessed we had always been with such love through dedicated family and friends. We realized it was the goodness of our Holy God that provided the visits on those days.

YOUR THOUGHTS

✓ Tell about a critical time in your life when you received God's blessing by being with friends.

✓ Why is fellowship with others so vital in our lives?

_____

_____

_____

_____

_____

_____

_____

_____

_____

GOD'S WORDS

❖ *Therefore, as God's chosen people, holy and dearly loved, clothe yourselves with compassion, kindness, humility, gentleness, and patience. Bear with each other and forgive one another if any of you has a grievance against someone. Forgive as the Lord forgave you. And over all these virtues put on love, which binds them all together in perfect unity.* Colossians 3:12-14

❖ *Friends, let us love one another, for love comes from God. Everyone who loves has been born of God and knows God.* I John 4:7

❖ *As a father has compassion on his children, so the LORD has compassion on those who fear him, or he knows how we are formed, he remembers that we are dust.* Psalm 103:13

❖ *Through Jesus, therefore, let us continually offer to God a sacrifice of praise—the fruit of lips that openly profess his name.* Hebrews 13:15

HYMNS FOR TODAY

 Hymn of Praise (Gaither Vocal Band)

God, I thank you this morning for healing my husband and for giving him the most glorious birthday.

My husband's favorite Bible verse was John 14:27, which speaks of the peace Jesus leaves with us. And Max lived a life filled with God's peace until his very last breath. His favorite hymns were *Amazing Grace* and *I Can Only Imagine*. Because of God's peace, His grace and the promise of heaven, my husband was ready to meet his Lord and Savior.

On Sunday morning, October 11, 2020, my husband went peacefully to his eternal rest during his sleep. It was also his birthday. His recent days had been filled with immense pain, primarily because of his bladder cancer. My son and I spent days caring for him, along with nurses who came in to help. Sometimes, we had to call to get extra help to care for him. Even though the days were difficult, God gave me what I needed. I praise Him for His peace and His provision!

The sadness of the day was that my beloved was gone, but the excitement was that his "gift" was that he was entering the glory of heaven on his birthday. Our Life Group at church wanted us to join them on Zoom so they could sing "Happy Birthday" to Max. I sent a text to one of them, informing them that we couldn't do the Zoom and that I would call her later. He had already gone.

I later learned that our friends still sang to him; I hope he saw and heard them. They all loved and respected him. He had been teaching our Sunday morning group for many years and enjoyed all of them. Interestingly, the hospice nurse stated the time of death was 9:40 a.m. That was the time he was usually getting ready to teach the Bible lesson on Sunday mornings.

For eighteen months, doctors had worked so diligently to heal his blood disease. And Max had not suffered until the last few days. God had His hand on my husband. Max was at peace with all that happened in his life, and he knew that he would spend eternity in heaven. His strong faith had been an encouragement to me and our family and friends during those months.

YOUR THOUGHTS

✓ What do you think "loving life" means? What is death?
✓ How do you see "life" and "death" in God's plan?

_____

_____

_____

_____

_____

_____

_____

_____

_____

_____

GOD'S WORD

❖ *Peace I leave with you, my peace I give to you. I do not give to you as the world gives. Do not let your hearts be troubled and do not be afraid.* John 14:27

❖ *If we live, we live to the Lord and if we die, we die to the Lord. So, whether we live or whether we die, we belong to the Lord.* Romans 14:8

❖ *Jesus said to her, "I am the resurrection and the life. The one who believes in me will live, even though they die; and whoever lives by believing in me will never die. Do you believe this?"* John 11:25-26

HYMNS FOR TODAY

 I Can Only Imagine (Bart Millard, 1999),
Amazing Grace (John Newton, 1779)

BEING THANKFUL FOR GOD'S PEACE, PROMISES, PRESENCE AND GOODNESS

Thank you, Lord for filling us with Your joy and peace that becomes a true witness to so many people.

During my husband's last days and as we were planning his burial and memorial services, our family received many texts, calls, and messages. They talked about the profound influence his Christian way of life had on many people. People from all aspects of his life, including friends, neighbors, and coworkers, shared their thoughts and experiences. And oh, how much we loved and appreciated all our friends at First Baptist Church in Conroe, where Max had so faithfully taught the Bible on Sunday mornings for over twenty years.

Thinking about my husband's humble, quiet, easy-going life, I knew that he had just lived life as God planned. Max would readily tell you he was just a sinner saved by God's grace. It was not in his nature to brag or boast of what he did for others or his earthly accomplishments. It was in his whole being to daily study God's Word, live out the Word, and love others. That is why he had so much joy and peace in his life.

Seeing so many people's responses to his Christian influence on their lives, I chose to have a video of the song "I Then Shall Live" played at the end of his service. Primarily, I hoped that it would inspire all of us as we carried on with our lives. At a Bill Gaither concert years ago, Max and I were introduced to this moving song that resonated with us because of its message.

No one was talking about the successes that my husband had had as a high school coach or in national fishing tournaments. People were only focusing on his Christian influence. In Max's work with Fellowship Christian Athletes, he often would tell groups that his happiness was not based on winning games but on his relationship with Jesus Christ. And that is how he could live a life that touched so many people. It is just a reminder to us that those earthly treasures and accomplishments mean nothing compared to a life lived with God's peace, joy, and love for others.

YOUR THOUGHTS

✓ How do you see yourself "living" your life these days? Is it by God's standards or by worldly standards?

✓ Is your life a witness of your Lord to others?

_____

_____

_____

_____

_____

_____

_____

_____

_____

_____

GOD'S WORD

❖ *I have been crucified with Christ and I no longer live, but Christ lives in me. The life I live in the body, I live by faith in the Son of God, who loved me and gave himself for me.* Galatians 2:20

❖ *I pray that out of his glorious riches he may strengthen you with power through his Spirit in your inner being, so that Christ may dwell in your hearts through faith. And I pray that you, being rooted and established in love, may have power, together with all the saints, to grasp how wide and long and high and deep is the love of Christ, and to know this love that surpasses knowledge, that you may be filled to the measure of all the fullness of God.* Ephesians 3:16-19

❖ *Now to him who is able to do immeasurably more than all we ask or imagine, according to his power that is at work within us, to him be glory in the church and in Christ Jesus throughout all generations, forever and forever! Amen.* Ephesians 3:20

HYMNS FOR TODAY

 I Am Just a Sinner Saved by Grace (William Gaither),
I Then Shall Live (Gloria Gaither, 1981)

O Lord, thank You for such great love through Your people. I am assured that in this new journey, I can trust in Your promises.

God blessed me with some dear family members and close longtime friends to be with me on the day of my husband's burial. It was a wonderful "Celebration of Life" service for him in the church sanctuary where we had worshipped for twenty-four years. Our long-time friend Holly provided beautiful piano music. Our ministers and church staff graciously were there for me and conducted such a beautiful service. Many people attended with masks and social distancing, while countless others watched the live-stream service.

The following day, my body was exhausted. I spent the entire day resting and longing for my husband's company. All the relatives had gone home except for our son, who planned to stay with me throughout the holidays. Having never lived alone, I was grateful for him being with me. I knew I did not need to be alone in my house at that time. Throughout the next few days, my son and I remained at home because of the pandemic, which made it challenging not to be around other people.

I cried many tears, talked to my husband often, and experienced God's faithfulness in caring for me. Friends continued to text or call just at the correct times when I needed someone. Writing numerous thank-you notes was a blessing, and it amazed me. It warmed my heart to see my husband's legacy being remembered through monetary gifts to the Ladies' Friendship Organization Scholarship fund and the donation of Bibles to the Gideons' ministry in his honor. What a delight to see the generosity, knowing how much Max had loved God's Holy Bible and had spent his lifetime working with students.

God had blessed our fifty-year marriage and filled it with so many precious memories; I tried to focus on my thankfulness even as my heart ached and tears flowed. God would be with me during the next few days and months. One of the great promises of the Bible is that He will never leave us or forsake us, and I continue to cling to that promise daily.

YOUR THOUGHTS

✓ Recall a time in your life when you experienced huge adjustments.
✓ Which of God's promises were influential in your life during that time?

_____

_____

_____

_____

_____

_____

_____

_____

_____

_____

GOD'S WORD

❖ *Blessed are those that mourn, for they will be comforted.* Matthew 5:4

❖ *God has given us his great and precious promises, so that through them you may participate in the divine nature, having escaped the corruption in the world caused by evil desires.* 2 Peter 1:4

❖ *The LORD watches over you, the LORD is your shade at your right hand; the sun will not harm you by day, nor the moon by night.* Psalm 121:5

❖ *God is faithful, who has called you into fellowship with His Son, Jesus Christ our Lord.* I Corinthians 1:9

HYMNS FOR TODAY

 Standing on the Promises (Russell K. Carter, 1886)

> *Thank you, God, for my husband, who so lovingly held my hand for fifty years.*

The one thing I really missed the most was holding hands with my husband. For many years, we made sure we went to bed at night at the same time. We would lie there holding hands until one of us went to sleep. Max always held my hand every time we prayed together at home and at church. We often walked along together, holding hands. I felt so loved and proud to have a husband who loved me deeply and had continued to hold my hand throughout our fifty years together.

Often, my thoughts focused on how God had faithfully held our hands during my husband's illness and the long, lonely days of the pandemic, showing us His love and comfort. There is just something exceptional about the touch of a hand that gives us comfort, love, and joy that flows from God. Many people are blessed to have family members who hold their hand or a special friend who is always there to hold a hand when times are tough.

My husband and I enjoyed holding hands because of our love for each other, which does not even compare to how deeply God loves us. As life continued, I needed my precious Lord to hold my hand in the lonely days ahead. What a blessing to know God's presence and to be aware of His holding my hand every day in all my situations!

YOUR THOUGHTS

✓ Tell about a parent, spouse, or friend who has held your hand in life.
✓ Why do you think a personal touch can be so uplifting?

_____

_____

_____

_____

_____

_____

_____

_____

GOD'S WORD

❖ *Because you are my help, I sing in the shadow of your wings, I cling to you; your right hand upholds me.* Psalm 63:7-8

❖ *Shouts of joy and victory resound in the tents of the righteous: "The LORD's right hand has done mighty things! The Lord's right hand is lifted high; the LORD's right hand has done mighty things!"* Psalm 118:15

❖ *For I am the LORD your God who takes hold of your right hand and says to you, Do not be fear; I will help you.* Isaiah 41:13

HYMNS FOR TODAY

Precious Lord Take My Hand (Thomas A. Dorsey, 1938)

Jesus, Hold My Hand (Albert E. Brumley, 1993)

> *Lord, my heart is full of gratitude for blessing us through Your people.*

Two simple words, "thank you," are so effective and represent the appreciation of a grateful heart. We all know people who are constantly saying "Thank you" to others and find that a very uplifting gesture. My husband used those two words often and expected someone to respond with, "You are welcome." Every time a nurse or doctor helped him, he always told them, "Thank you." Even to the last nurse who came to help him manage his pain—in his weakened voice, he made sure he told her, "Thank you."

I wrote many "thank you" notes to our loved ones who supported us during Max's illness and passing. I continued to be in awe of how God blessed us through many loving acts of people. My heart wanted to make sure that I acknowledged all who gave to us, for I viewed them as instruments of our Lord. I continuously voice my "thanks" to God for His loving and giving through these people.

YOUR THOUGHTS

✓ How do you see God in the generous actions of others?
✓ How do you express your gratitude to God and others?

_____

_____

_____

_____

_____

_____

_____

_____

_____

GOD'S WORD

❖ *You will be enriched in every way so that you can be generous on every occasion, and through us your generosity will result in thanksgiving to God.*
2 Corinthians 9:11

❖ *Give thanks to the LORD, for he is good, for his steadfast love endures forever.*
Psalm 107:1

❖ *What shall I return to the LORD for all his goodness to me? I will lift up the cup of salvation and call on the name of the LORD. I will fulfill my vows to the LORD in the presence of all his people.* Psalm 116:12-14

❖ *For from him, and through him and for him are all things. To him be the glory forever! Amen!* Romans 11:36

HYMNS FOR TODAY

 My Tribute (Andraé Crouch, 1971)

Thank You, God, that I can always boldly enter Your throne room because I so need You every hour of every day.

During the days of becoming a widow, I learned quickly that there were so many things to deal with, such as business decisions, life insurance, retirement income, and much more. When making necessary phone calls, I often was put "on hold" and endured several minutes of silence or listening to music. During those moments, I often told God, "Thank you for never putting me on hold!" To be more productive during those times of being on hold, I prayed for my friends and family who were ill or going through challenging times.

Occasionally, during busy workdays, when I felt frustrated and uncertain, a friend would call and check up on me. On a particular day, I was irritated by several phone calls when, unexpectedly, my friend Deitra called to see how I was doing. We have always enjoyed conversation and laughter, and we have encouraged each other in our spiritual lives.

What a blessing she was that day! Having a phone conversation with a supportive friend was really helpful for me then. It gave me time to relax and then get back to the business, and I then had more peace and understanding about it.

Yes, God never puts us on hold and, through His Spirit, gives us encouraging words from a friend that helps us see better and understand our situations and concerns. In all my days of worship *under the shade trees* or in any other place, I continue to need my God and have the assurance that He is with me every hour of every day.

YOUR THOUGHTS

- ✓ Recall a time when a phone call or business dealing frustrated you.
- ✓ What do you do to handle such situations?
- ✓ How does God help us during those times?

_____

_____

_____

_____

_____

_____

_____

_____

_____

_____

GOD'S WORD

- ❖ *The LORD is my light and my salvation, whom shall I fear? The LORD is the stronghold of my life; of whom shall I be afraid?* Psalm 27:1

- ❖ *Humble yourselves under the mighty hand of God so that in the proper time he may exalt you, casting all your anxieties on him, because he cares for you.* I Peter 5:6-7

- ❖ *As the Father has loved me, so have I loved you. Now remain in my love.* John 15:9

- ❖ *Let us with confidence draw near to the throne of grace that we may receive mercy and find grace to help in time of need.* Hebrews 4:16

HYMNS FOR TODAY

 I Need Thee Every Hour (Annie S. Hawks, 1872 and Robert Lowry, 1871)

> *Lord, please help me in my grieving and renew my strength.*

I found it easy to grieve alone in my bedroom and to focus so much on missing my husband. Our county was still under the COVID restrictions; it seemed that the number of cases had risen. I was inclined to remain at home, creating my own little world and cherishing moments with my son.

After a while, I realized my joy has always been serving others as God led. I continued to read and study God's word and spend more time in worship with Him daily. Additionally, I returned to writing and reached out to those I knew were in pain or feeling isolated. I met with a few women at church to plan some mission outreach.

My strong desire was to let God lead me in "being" His servant again. I knew I needed to reach out to my ESL friends and some new ladies in our congregation. A scripture came to mind: The "joy of the LORD is my strength" and I felt a renewal in my spirit.

During my time of loss and sorrow, I realized that this was a chance for me to put into practice everything I had ever learned about God. All my quiet times and Bible studies had prepared me for these days, and I had to dedicate myself to allowing the Holy Spirit to be alive in me. I also knew that my life was not about what *I* was doing but about what *God* was doing in my life as I depended on Him.

YOUR THOUGHTS

✓ Why is it so easy to focus on one's grief or problems?
✓ How does the faithfulness of God's Holy Word help you in your daily life?

_____

_____

_____

_____

_____

_____

_____

_____

_____

_____

GOD'S WORD

❖ *Those who hope in the LORD will renew their strength. They will soar on wings like eagles; they will run and not grow weary, they will walk and not be faint.* Isaiah 40:31

❖ *Now she who is really a widow (left alone) trusts in God and continues in supplications and prayers night and day.* I Timothy 5:5

❖ *Therefore, since we are surrounded by such a great cloud of witnesses, let us throw off everything that hinders and the sin that so easily entangles. And let us run with perseverance the race marked out for us, fixing our eyes on Jesus, the author and perfecter of faith. For the joy set before Him, Jesus endured the cross, scorning its shame, and sat down at the right hand of the throne of God. Consider him who endured such opposition from sinners, so that you will not grow weary and lose heart.* Hebrews 12: 1-3

HYMNS FOR TODAY

 Day by Day (Caroline V. Sandell-Berg, sung by Chris Tomlin)

> *God, I thank You that You never change. You are always the same and ready to guide us through life as we experience so many changes.*

Throughout 2020, I thought about all the changes that had taken place not only in my life but also in our entire society. Lives that went from good health to illnesses and some even death. There are so many changes in our daily routines, our social life, and perhaps our spiritual lives. There were changes in family gatherings and how we celebrated holidays. The pandemic has affected every area of our lives.

When I examined the impact of those changes on myself, I quickly noticed a significant transformation in my daily routine. The other half of me was gone. I no longer had my husband to share conversations, spend time with him, eat meals together, and enjoy his company. Adjusting to those changes was the hardest thing that I had ever done.

It was essential to realize that I had not changed; I was still the person God created me to be, just no longer a loving wife. I still had a Holy God who lived in me and continued to teach me many things each day through the Holy Spirit. I knew I was still here, and my faithfulness to God would continue to be so important in my life. I had children and grandchildren to love. As they live in other states, I continued to be thankful that modern technology provided us opportunities to stay in constant touch with each other.

I focused on the thought that our circumstances change many times throughout life, but as Christians, we are assured that our Holy God *never* changes. He continues to love and guide us through all the changes and challenges of our lives. He is still the one who loves us unconditionally, provides for us, and gives us peace during the difficult times of life.

YOUR THOUGHTS

✓ What changes have been the most challenging for you in recent years?
✓ Have any changes or challenges affected your faith in God?

_____

_____

_____

_____

_____

_____

_____

_____

_____

_____

GOD'S WORD

❖ *"I the LORD do not change. So you, the descendants of Jacob, are not destroyed. Ever since the time of your ancestors, you have turned away from my decrees and have not kept them. Return to me, and I will return to you," says the LORD Almighty.* Malachi 3:6-7

❖ *The grass withers and the flowers fall, but the word of our God will stand forever.* Isaiah 40:8

❖ *Jesus Christ is the same yesterday and today and forever.* Hebrews 13:8

❖ " I am the Alpha and the Omega," says the Lord God, "who is, and who was, and who is to come, the Almighty." Revelation 1:8

❖ Every good and perfect gift is from above, coming down from the Father of the heavenly lights, who does not change like shifting shadows. James 1:17

HYMNS FOR TODAY

 Hold to God's Unchanging Hand (Jennie Wilson)

> *God, I thank You for*
> *Your goodness to us.*

As people all over the world were under the influence of the 2020 pandemic, it seemed to be challenging to see any good in their days. Many families faced agonizing situations with the virus or loss of income. Those who were part of lockdowns suffered from being alone and not being with family.

Many suffered from medical conditions alone without family. The loss of life seemed especially hard for families. People focused on the uncertainty of life and the confusion of how to handle all the problems brought on by the pandemic.

Even as I write this, COVID is still the central issue of the day. Many people continue to say, "God is still in control." As I look back over the time which totally changed our way of life, I can still see the goodness of God.

As my son and I spent Thanksgiving week with my sister's family, we enjoyed watching the young people of the family play their guitars and sing about the goodness of God. Some of them had had the virus and survived. It was so refreshing to see the youth praising God for His loving care over all of us.

Acknowledging God and His goodness gives us hope, shows our faith in Him, and, above all, honors the One who gives us such an abundance of the good things of life, joy, and peace.

YOUR THOUGHTS

✓ How did you see the goodness of God during the pandemic or another challenging time of life?
✓ Were you able to acknowledge that goodness verbally to others?

_____

_____

_____

_____

_____

_____

_____

_____

_____

GOD'S WORD

❖ *The LORD is good, a refuge in time of trouble. He cares for those who trust in him.* Nahum 1:7

❖ *How abundant are the good things that you have stored up for those who fear you, that you bestow in the sight of all, on those who take refuge in you!* Psalm 31:19

❖ *Taste and see that the LORD is good, blessed is the one who takes refuge in him.* Psalm 34:8

❖ *For the LORD God is a sun and shield; the LORD bestows favor and honor; no good thing does he withhold from those whose walk is blameless.* Psalm 84:11

❖ *The LORD is good to all; he has compassion on all that he has made.* Psalm 145:9

HYMNS FOR TODAY

 The Goodness of God (Jenn Johnson, Jason Ingram, Ben Fielding, Ed Cash, 2019)

> *Thank you, Lord, for your help with the exasperations of earthly situations.*

The constant need to make decisions without my husband's input would occasionally frustrate me. My son was willing to help in many ways. For example, he planned to sell my husband's pickup truck for me. One Sunday afternoon, he met a man who offered cash for a reasonable price, but then there was a problem. So, that transaction did not take place.

The next day, my son was meeting with another prospective buyer. While he was gone, I spent time at my piano playing and singing hymns. I finally just broke down and cried out to God that I was tired of all the legal and physical things. Soon, the phone rang, and my son told me that a young man wanted to purchase the vehicle that night. Through texts and emails, my friends provided quick help in guiding me on what to do with the correct paperwork, and we finished it before meeting for the sale and transfer of the title that night.

God knows our needs and frustrations so well. I had faith that God would take care of selling the vehicle, but again, His faithfulness was such a big blessing. The young man who purchased the pickup gave us more cash than the first offer. And the blessing of selling it in two days showed me God's faithfulness in *His* timing. I continued to give thanks to God for all the ways He is in control of my life's situations.

YOUR THOUGHTS

- ✓ Have you seen God's faithfulness in your life this week?
- ✓ Have you given thanks to Him?

_____

_____

_____

_____

_____

_____

_____

_____

GOD'S WORD

❖ *Praise be to God, who has not rejected my prayer or withheld his love from me!*
   Psalm 66:20

❖ *Jesus said, "If you believe, you will receive whatever you ask for in prayer."*

   Matthew 21:22

❖ *Trust in the LORD with all your heart, do not lean on your own understanding;*
   in all your ways submit to him and he will make your paths straight.
   Proverbs 3:5-6

❖ *He replied, "Because you have so little faith. Truly I tell you, if you have faith as*
   small as a mustard seed, you can say to this mountain, 'Move from here to there,'
   and it will move. Nothing will be impossible with you." Matthew 17:20

❖ *The Lord has done great things for us, and we are filled with joy.* Psalm 126:3

HYMNS FOR TODAY

 Give Thanks (Henry Smith, 1978)

PRAISING GOD FOR HIS LOVE, GUIDANCE, PROVISION AND COMFORT

> *Father in heaven, I praise You for Your love revealed in the true meaning of Christmas.*

As days went by and more people seemed to have contracted the virus, I continued to stay at home except for necessary trips to the pharmacy, grocery store, or drive-thru for fast food. I noticed on social media that many people were going out shopping, eating at restaurants, attending events, and being with family. Others avoided any possibility of being exposed to the virus.

I finally put up my Christmas tree, which is always filled with family memories and focused on the birth of Jesus, our Savior. This made me realize how much I longed for the company of other family members and my church community. Watching the church Christmas concert brought peace and joy to my heart as I witnessed my choir and orchestra friends unite to deliver stunning performances that celebrated God's love and the birth of the Messiah for all humanity.

Often, I sat at my piano playing hymns and Christmas carols. There are so many songs of worship for Christmas. One day while playing the simple song *Jesus Loves Me,* I thought about how valid its message is today as it was thousands of years ago. Playing the song *Away in a Manger* reminded me of my high school days when I played the piano for a preschool mission group on Monday afternoons. The children's favorite song to sing every week, all year long, was *Away in a Manger*! Yes, the story of Jesus' birth, which we celebrate at Christmas, lives in the heart of every believer throughout the entire year.

One of my favorite hymns is *O Holy Night;* I continue to be so grateful for the Holiness of God coming to earth because of His great love for a sinful world. My prayer is that more people would believe in the Christ Child and humbly worship Him because Christmas is about God's love, a love that is shared with others every day of every year.

YOUR THOUGHTS

✓ How do you see Christmas as God's love for the world?

✓ What are some distractions that keep people from the truth of Christmas?

_____

_____

_____

_____

_____

_____

_____

_____

_____

_____

_____

GOD'S WORD

❖ *But when the set time had fully come, God sent His Son, born of a woman, born under the law to redeem those under the law that we might receive adoption of sonship.* Galatians 4:4-5

❖ *This is how God showed us his love among us: He sent his one and only Son into the world that we might live through Him. This is love: not that we loved God, but that he loved us and sent his Son as an atoning sacrifice for our sins.* I John 4:9-10

❖ *For God so loved the world that he gave his only Son that whoever believes in him shall not perish but have eternal life. For God did not send his Son into the world to condemn the world, but to save the world through him.* John 3:16-17

HYMNS FOR TODAY

 O Holy Night (Author, Placide Cappeau, 1847, Translator, John S. Dwight)

Father, I continue to praise You for the signs and wonders in the heavens that show Your mighty power.

The week of Christmas 2020 offered a spectacular sight to the world: a brilliantly shining Christmas star and a full moon. It was really not a star, but the conjunction of the two planets Saturn and Jupiter, and, to our eyes on Earth, appeared as one bright star. This was covered in the news, and people observed it during the night. Our family sat outside on Christmas night by a firepit at dusk and enjoyed seeing the wonders of the heavenly skies at sunset and beyond. Such beauty! Such splendor, knowing it was of God!

Many people were saying it was a sign from God to assure us of His care and sovereignty following the darkness of the pandemic. It was a bright star that led the Wise Men from the East to find the Christ child on that first Christmas. My prayer was that many people who were looking at the bright sign in the sky this Christmas would decide to seek Jesus and accept Him as the Savior of the world. Jesus had brought hope and light to a world of darkness and continues to do so. Oh, the beauty and wonder of the night sky during this Christmas season!

Yes, God used the star to show the first coming of the Messiah. He will also use signs in the sky to announce the second coming of Jesus. O, the glory and the power of God in the heavens to reveal to us who He is!

YOUR THOUGHTS

✓ Were you able to witness the Christmas star?
✓ How can the heavenly signs influence our faith?

_____

_____

_____

_____

_____

_____

_____

_____

_____

_____

GOD'S WORD

❖ Read Luke 2:1-20

❖ *After Jesus was born in Bethlehem in Judea, during the time of King Herod, Magi from the east came to Jerusalem and asked, "Where is the one who has been born King of the Jews? We saw his star when it rose and have come to worship him."* Matthew 2:1-2

❖ *But in those days, following that distress, the sun will be darkened; and the moon will not give light; the stars will fall from the sky, and the heavenly bodies will be shaken. At that time, people will see the Son of Man coming in clouds with great power and glory. And he will send his angels and gather his elect from the four winds, from the ends of the earth to the ends of the heavens.* Mark 13:24-27

HYMNS FOR TODAY

 Beautiful Star of Bethlehem (R. Fisher Boyce, 1938)

> *God, I pray for the spiritual healing of our people. I praise You for provisions to stand against the evil one.*

At the beginning of the new year, 2021, there seemed to be so much division in our country over a variety of issues. I questioned what pleases our God. I canceled my TV cable, so I couldn't keep up with everything that was going on, which turned out to be a good thing for me. During those times with God, I felt His peace and the assurance that He was still in control.

Our enemies are not of a physical force, but of a spiritual nature. Satan has blinded the eyes of so many, so they cannot see God's love through Jesus. Yes, Christians need to pray for the spiritual healing of our country. I prayed that we, as Christians, would be diligent in standing up for the teachings of Jesus Christ and love others as He taught us to do. Yes, we need to be strong in standing in Christ alone and being a witness to who He is in our lives.

YOUR THOUGHTS

✓ What do you see as enemies of our faith in God?
✓ What is your attitude towards these enemies?

_____

_____

_____

_____

_____

_____

_____

_____

_____

_____

GOD'S WORD

❖ *"But to you who are listening I say: Love your enemies, do good to those who hate you, bless those who curse you, pray for those who mistreat you."* Luke 6:27-28

❖ *Finally, be strong in the Lord and his mighty power. Put on the full armor of God so that you can take your stand against the devil's schemes. For our struggle is not against flesh and blood but against the rulers, against the authorities, against the powers of the dark world and against the spiritual forces of evil in the heavenly realms.* Ephesians 6:10-12

❖ *Be alert and of sober mind. Your enemy the devil prowls around like a roaring lion looking for someone to devour. Resist him, standing firm in the faith, because you know that the family of believers throughout the world is undergoing the same kind of sufferings.* I Peter 5:8-9

❖ Read Ephesians 6:14:14 -17. Make a list of the necessary armor of God.

HYMNS FOR TODAY

 Stand Up, Stand Up for Jesus (George Duffield, 1858)

> *Thank you, God, for blessing me with Your guidance in the plans You have for me.*

Over that final year of my husband's illness, my life had experienced a multitude of changes. I remained at home because of COVID. But there was a deep loneliness, and I needed to be with people. Ministry opportunities had always kept me busy, but that was no longer the case.

One morning, during my Bible study and prayer time, I strongly felt the power of the Holy Spirit with me. Crying out to God, I asked that He please show me what He had next in my life. About an hour later, I looked at my email and found a sweet note from a friend who was the director of our First Baptist Church Academy.

Joni asked me to consider working three mornings a week at FBA. As I sat weeping with joy, I knew this was God speaking to me. After much prayer and discussing the specifics of the job, I accepted it. My dear friend Mary Margaret had held this position for several years. But because of failing health, she could no longer work, so I wanted to do this as God was leading and for Mary Margaret.

Once again, I was in awe of God hearing my cry and showing me His plan for the next few months. Since I had worked at FBA a few years earlier, it was like returning home. All the church staff welcomed me and offered their encouragement, as did my new friends at the academy. I felt at peace with my decision and trusted God to continue His care over me, as I knew He was lovingly guiding me through this.

YOUR THOUGHTS

✓   Tell about a time when God stepped in and gave you a new job or opportunity for service.

✓   How did you see God in that plan?

_____

_____

_____

_____

_____

_____

_____

_____

_____

_____

GOD'S WORD

❖   *"When the Advocate comes, whom I will send to you from the Father--the Spirit of truth who goes out from the Father--he will bear testify of me."* John 15:26

❖   *Create in me a pure heart, O God, and renew a steadfast spirit within me. Do not cast me from your presence and take your Holy Spirit from me. Restore to me the joy of your salvation and grant me a willing spirit to sustain me.* Psalm 51:10-12

❖   *You guide me with your counsel, and afterward, you will take me into glory.* Psalm 73:24

❖   *For this God is our God for ever and ever; he will be our guide even to the end.* Psalm 48:14

❖ *This is what the LORD says-- your Redeemer, the Holy One of Israel: "I am the LORD your God, who teaches you what is best for you, who directs you in the way you should go."* Isaiah 48:17

❖ *The Lord will guide you always; he will satisfy your needs in a sun scorched land and will strengthen your frame. You will be like a well-watered garden, like a spring whose waters never fail.* Isaiah 58:11

HYMNS FOR TODAY

 All the Way My Savior Leads Me (Fanny Crosby, 1875)

A horrific snowstorm hit Texas in February 2021, which was very unusual. Being aware of the forecast, I took steps to prepare. When the snow and ice came with extremely low temperatures, I was in for a shock and lost electricity, as most people did. Survival meant staying in bed with layers and layers of clothes and blankets for two days. Keeping in contact with my family through my cell phone was very important, but soon, my battery died. I was so miserable and so cold, and I knew that many other people were experiencing the same misery.

I was totally alone! It was disappointing that my neighbors, who were out and about, didn't bother to check on me. My inner being told me I could lie there for days in deep sadness and depression, or I could totally trust in God, as I had often done during the hard times of life. Every time I would get up and look out a window, I would see a lonely bird, which reminded me that God was taking care of it and would take care of me.

Because of the ice on my driveway, I was concerned about trying to get to my car. I just kept talking to God and finally realized that I must try to reach out to a neighbor. By early Tuesday afternoon, the ice was not too bad right outside my door, so I carefully stepped out and noticed my neighbor Susan in her yard. I called out to her that I needed my phone charged. She walked to me and then helped me walk through the snow to her house so I could get warm in her car and charge my phone. Later, she walked me back to my house and brought a shovel to clear a path to my car so I could get to it when I needed to charge my phone and get warm. What a blessing she was that day and has been to me for several days since!

While I was in bed trying to stay warm, I couldn't help but gaze at the wall decor in my room that says, "God is Faithful." My mind was occupied with memories of how God had consistently shown His faithfulness to me throughout the years. In my heart,

I knew He would send help to me. While I was suffering physically, I kept listening to God for His guidance in ways to keep myself safe and trusting that He would send help.

And He was so faithful to do so! As I look back on that time, I realize God was telling me to continue to keep my faith in Him constant. And it is okay to ask others for help, which allows God to work through them. Also, as the Holy Spirit leads me, I need to reach out to others with their physical and spiritual needs.

YOUR THOUGHTS

✓ What were your major concerns during an unusual weather event (like a snowstorm) or another natural disaster?
✓ How did you see God help you deal with those issues?

_____

_____

_____

_____

_____

_____

_____

_____

_____

_____

GOD'S WORD

❖ *But the Lord is faithful, and he will strengthen you and protect you from the evil one.* 2 Thessalonians 3:3

❖ *Your word, LORD, is eternal; it stands firm in the heavens. Your faithfulness continues through all generations; you have established the earth, and it endures.* Psalm 119:89-90

❖ *Each of you should look not only to your own interests but also to the interests of others.* Philippians 2:4

HYMNS FOR TODAY

 My Faith Looks Up to Thee (Ray Palmer, 1830)

> *I praise You, God, for taking care of all my needs as You see and understand my total being.*

During the terrible snowstorm and the days that followed, I was seeking God for His care. After getting my phone recharged, I called my children, my sisters, and dear friends who had been trying to keep in touch with me. I also called to check on my friend Sarah in Conroe. She and her husband had not lost their electricity at any time. They wanted to drive out to my house and take me to their home so I could stay with them. They picked me up in Danny's large truck, and we headed to Conroe from the lake.

It was terrific to get a hot shower, eat a good hot meal, and be with such caring friends. Reading and writing occupied the time. Talking and visiting with Sarah and Danny were the highlights of those three days. I had not been with people in so long, and I did not realize how much I needed it.

Joyously, I thanked God for my days of warmth and fellowship with my friends. Sarah and I always have fun sharing "teacher" stories. In the evenings, after dinner, Danny would read aloud chapters from the book *Begin Again* by Max Lucado. I discussed with God once more the new beginnings He had for me in the upcoming days, inspired by the book.

As my friends drove me home on Saturday, I continued to pray that my house would be safe with no damage, such as frozen pipes. As we entered my house, we found that all was well with the heat on, the water faucets all working, and the sun shining outside. My greatest praise to God was how refreshed I felt, having been with friends. I spent the afternoon calling and texting family and friends to say that I was safely home and that my house had no damage. That night, in warmth and singing praises to my

Lord, I thanked God for His loving care through the help of my friends. He had (once again) *held me fast* while supplying all my physical, mental, and spiritual needs.

YOUR THOUGHTS

✓ Have you felt God taking care of you during the physical storms of life?
✓ Did God use people to help you or give you the opportunity to help others?

_____

_____

_____

_____

_____

_____

_____

_____

_____

_____

GOD'S WORD

❖ *But as for me, I am poor and needy; may the LORD think of me. You are my help and my deliverer. You are my God, do not delay.* Psalm 40:17

❖ *Share with the Lord's people who are in need. Practice hospitality.* Romans 12:13

❖ *Carry each other's burdens, and in this way, you will fulfill the law of Christ.* Galatians 6:2

❖ *Praise be to the God and Father of our Lord Jesus Christ. the Father of compassion and the God of all comfort, who comforts us in all our troubles; so that we can comfort those in any trouble with the comfort we ourselves have received from God.* 2 Corinthians 1:3-4

❖ *For the LORD takes delight in his people; he crowns the humble with victory.* Psalm 149:4

HYMNS FOR TODAY

 He Will Hold Me Fast (Ada R. Habershon, 1906)

> *Thank you, God, for blessing me with memories of loved ones and their faithfulness to You.*

Living alone now and working three mornings a week, I recognized God's intervention in every aspect of my life. While attending the funeral of my friend Mary Margaret on February 24, 2021, I thought of how God had blessed the two of us—with a friendship that began at First Baptist Academy as teachers. Later, we could serve together on the Pastor Search Committee and share in Bible studies and women's ministry.

My friend is no longer with me, but I am blessed with memories, particularly the memories of her constant contact during my husband's illness for nearly two years. She was always such a gracious, caring friend—not only to me, but to countless others. Working in her classroom at First Baptist Academy, her sweet spirit always surrounded me, and I cherished the memories of how she treated children and parents with love and kindness. She was a beautiful lady genuinely filled with God's Spirit, and so used in the Kingdom for His glory.

And I shall never forget her praying with me on the phone as I sat *under a shade tree* at the hospital when I told her of my writing this study. Except for my husband, she was the primary person to whom I revealed my plans for writing *Under the Shade Tree.* What a blessing she continues to be, as so many of her family and friends remember her faithfulness to God!

Mary Margaret and I shared a lot, especially during our prayer times in the church library's workroom, which we referred to as our prayer closet. And such memories I treasure in my heart! Over those months, I realized how precious our memories are when we no longer have a loved one with us. My mind is always filled with memories, and I am grateful to God for the cherished moments I shared with my husband and friends who have left for heaven in the past year.

I have learned that in those memories, I am reminded of the strong faith of my loved ones and how their faith had been such a steady influence on their families and friends. What a blessing! What an honor to our Lord!

YOUR THOUGHTS

✓ Do you have memories of a friend who strongly affected your life for the better?
✓ What are some special memories you are making that can encourage someone spiritually?

_____

_____

_____

_____

_____

_____

_____

_____

_____

_____

GOD'S WORD

❖ *In everything set an example by doing what is good.* Titus 2:7

❖ *Be wise in the way you act toward outsiders; make the most of every opportunity. Let your conversation always be full of grace, seasoned with salt, so that you may know how to answer everyone.* Colossians 4:5-6

❖ *Charm is deceitful, and beauty is fleeting; but a woman who fears the LORD is to be praised. Honor her for all that her hands have done, and let her works praise her at the city gate.* Proverbs 31:30-31

❖ *The name of the righteous is used in blessings, but the name of the wicked will rot.* Proverbs 10:7

HYMNS FOR TODAY

 Precious Memories (J. B.F. Wright, 1925)

> *Dear Lord, I praise You as You comfort me in this journey of sorrow and grief.*

Throughout my journey of grief, loneliness filled my life. Evenings and weekends seemed to be the worst times. My neighbors were all preoccupied with their own families, so I had little contact with them. Yet, thankfully, they were only a phone call away if I needed them. Phone conversations and texts were so helpful.

Even months later, there would be several times a day that I would shed tears for about fifteen minutes. Sometimes, I would call my sister Rita, who was always an encouragement to me. Getting my first COVID vaccine in February was a very emotional experience. Being told of the death of another friend in our church, I lost all control of my emotions while seated in the medical facility after receiving the vaccine. Then I got in my car and cried for fifteen minutes and had to call my sister.

Part of my emotional breakdown was that I was in the place where my husband and I had spent so much time over the past two years. Yes, I was sitting *under a shade tree* at Houston Methodist. After arriving home safely on that cloudy afternoon, I sent a text to my sister. My concern about being alone for the second vaccine prompted me to call a friend. So, God blessed me three weeks later with the opportunity to ride with my friend Pat for that second vaccine. What a relief! And such a joy to be with my friend again in person!

Even in my loneliness, I did more Bible study and writing and trying to reach out to others. Playing my piano or watching Christian music on YouTube often lifted my spirits. I also thought about the sorrow and sadness that Jesus' disciples and other followers of Jesus must have experienced. They saw Him crucified, buried, rise again to speak to them, and then leave them again as He ascended to heaven.

Did they understand His sacrifice?
How did they go on without Him?
How did they grieve?
Did they feel alone without their Master, and were they confused?

Jesus sent (as promised) the Holy Spirit to them, which enabled them to move forward as God planned and continue with what Jesus had begun: spreading God's love to the world, which would give joy and peace to all nations. Jesus had also given them a hope of eternal life in heaven with him, where there would be no more death or mourning.

It was vital for me to understand that the grieving process takes a while; it is something that we all must go through in this life on earth. In my time of grief, I must depend on God to take care of me through the daily leadership of the Holy Spirit. I must always express God's joy and peace in my life daily and never be ashamed of my tears. Even as I missed my husband, he had always "lived in" God's joy and peace, and my memories of that were a constant source of encouragement for me.

YOUR THOUGHTS

✓ Can you name times when your grief was intense, and you felt so alone?
✓ Did you see God in those times?

_____

_____

_____

_____

_____

_____

_____

_____

_____

GOD'S WORD

❖ *Weeping may stay for the night, but rejoicing comes in the morning.* Psalm 30:5b

❖ *And I will pour out on the house of David and on the inhabitants of Jerusalem a spirit of grace and of supplication. They will look on me, the one they have pierced, and they will mourn for him as one mourns for an only child and grieve bitterly for him as one grieves for a firstborn son.* Zechariah 12:10

❖ *Jesus said, "Blessed are those who mourn, for they shall be comforted."* Matthew 5:4

❖ *Jesus said, "Very truly I tell you, you will weep and mourn while the world rejoices. You will grieve, but your grief will turn to joy."* John 16:20

❖ *He will wipe away every tear from their eyes. There shall be no more death or mourning or crying or pain, for the old order of things has passed away.* Revelation 21:4

HYMNS FOR TODAY

Joy Comes in the Morning (Mrs. M. M. Weinland)
Be Still My Soul (Kathrina von Schlegel, Jane Borthwick, Translator, 1855)

REJOICING

IN

LIFE

> *O, God, the blessings You are giving me through the love of these sweet children! It is so refreshing to my soul, and I thank You for a new shade tree in my life.*

Working at First Baptist Academy meant following mandatory mask and shield protocols while interacting with children. Every morning, teachers went outside to get our precious children out of their vehicles since no parents could enter the building. My duty was to put hand sanitizer in their sweet little hands as they came to the door. It was so cute to see them put their hands out, ready for me, as soon as they got out of their cars.

I worked with Pre-K children, helping them with their individual needs regarding the alphabet, numbers, and colors. A couple of them were reading a little, and it was enjoyable to listen to them as they were so proud of themselves. Working with these children is fantastic because they are loving, happy, and carefree at such a young age. Yes, God knew that my greatest need was to "get out of my house" to love these children and enjoy their loving me.

Working with young women who are passionate about caring for and teaching young children was another blessing. Yes, I needed those younger ladies in my life. We always began our day with prayer time. Every morning, as we stood outside to greet the kiddos, I looked intently at a nearby tree. It was ancient, with lots of scars and bumps, and appeared to have been through a lot during its life. Yet it was filled with new growth and big leaves for shade.

That tree continued to speak to me daily, a message that even during the rough times of life, God still uses us. Even when we are older, He will continue to do His work and His will in our lives. At every age and stage of life, we can humbly allow our God to live and love through us. He wants our willing hearts to be filled with His Spirit.

I am incredibly grateful for the months I spent at FBA, where I experienced God's love, teachings, and provision for my needs. And what a joy to know that I was there because one morning, I "cried out" to my God. He heard me and answered me in an incredible way! God's great love indeed lifted me out of my time of isolation and loneliness. I continue to rejoice in such a blessing!

YOUR THOUGHTS

✓ Is there a time when you cried out to God, and he answered you?
✓ How do you see God using men and women at every season of their lives?

GOD'S WORD

❖ *I waited patiently for the LORD; he turned to me and heard my cry. He lifted me out of the slimy pit, out of the mud and mire; he set my feet on a rock and gave me a firm place to stand. He put a new song in my mouth, a hymn of praise to our God.* Psalm 40:1-2

❖ *She speaks with wisdom, and faithful instruction is on her tongue.* Proverbs 31:26

❖ *Dear children, let us not love with words or speech but with actions and in truth. I* John 3:18

❖ *And now these three remain: faith, hope, and love. But the greatest of these is love.* I Corinthians 13:13

❖ *Humble yourselves, therefore, under God's mighty hand that he may lift you up in due time. I Peter 5:6*

HYMNS FOR TODAY

Love Lifted Me (James Rowe,1912)
I Stand Amazed, How Marvelous (Charles H. Gabriel,1905)

Father, thank You for the truth seen in Your creation, which reminds me of Your redemption plan for us through the sacrifice of Your Son and the power of the resurrection of our Christ.

During the week of Easter in 2021, I was invited to spend the weekend with my sister and her family in East Texas. I left my work at FBA in Conroe on Thursday at 11:30 a.m. My car was parked *under a shade tree,* so it was important to spend a few minutes of prayer time before leaving on my trip.

I drove for two hours with no music, just the silence in the car. I enjoyed the beauty of the green grassy fields, the budding of new growth on the trees, and the beautiful colors of the wildflowers on the roadside along the way. One area that I wouldn't say I like driving through is the road between Crockett and Alto. It is a long, lonely stretch. In recent years, a tornado demolished much of a beautiful forest along that road near Alto.

Approaching that area, I looked to the left of the highway and again saw the devastation of the horror of downed trees and logs scattered everywhere. But to my amazement, scattered among all that darkness were several lovely dogwood trees that seemed to shine with the white brightness of the glory of God. I thanked God for that scene and what it revealed about Him. What a powerful reminder of God's love and grace in the dark, ugly, sinful life on earth! Memories of my mother sharing the legend of the dogwood tree with me as a child flooded back.

The entire Easter weekend was blessed with family and worship from Friday evening to Sunday morning. My mother's favorite hymns were *In the Garden, The Old Rugged Cross,* as well as *Victory in Jesus,* were sung. These hymns were some we had often sung growing up, particularly at Easter, because they relate to death, resurrection, and Christ's victory over sin. One of my favorite hymns is *Because He Lives* which has been so comforting to me this year. I continue to praise God for His love and plan of salvation for us through a living Savior and Holy Spirit in our daily lives.

In my traveling, being with family, and experiencing the joy of worship through songs and God's Word, I truly sensed the presence of my living Lord with me throughout the weekend.

YOUR THOUGHTS

✓ How does the beauty of God's creation speak to you at Easter time?
✓ Do you have a special memory of God communicating with you at Easter?
✓ How do you spend time in worship during the Resurrection weekend?

_____

_____

_____

_____

_____

_____

_____

_____

_____

_____

GOD'S WORD

❖ Read John 18, 19, and 20. Look for things you have forgotten or never noticed before in these familiar verses.

❖ *Jesus said to him, "Because you have seen me, you have believed; blessed are those who have not seen and yet have believed."* John 20:29

HYMNS FOR TODAY

The Old Rugged Cross (George Bennard-1913)

Because He Lives (Gloria Gaither)

Lord, I rejoice in Your Spirit that shelters me safely in Your arms.

Throughout the spring and summer of 2021, I continued to experience roller coaster rides and storms in life. While making many decisions concerning house repairs, traveling, and church ministries, God continued to love me and lead me. Teaching Bible lessons to second graders in Vacation Bible School was a blessing. Planning a churchwide women's dinner kept me busy; I was excited to see a large group of our ladies gather for a time of fellowship and worship.

Traveling to the Dallas area one weekend gave me the opportunity to worship in my hometown church, First Baptist Church of Plano. There, we celebrated the church's 169th anniversary and the beginning of a new era, as God was leading them to build a new facility on the west side of the city. I enjoyed being with family and friends as we shared many memories.

Most of all, I was so thankful for how God blessed me through his people in that congregation many years ago. Those friends helped me grow spiritually, as well as supported me in college through prayers, encouraging words, and scholarships. While at the Plano church, I spent some time in the newly renovated small chapel, which was the sanctuary where Max and I had happily and solemnly spoken our wedding vows. What joyful emotions flooded my heart with memories of that beautiful day in my life!

On Tuesday morning, while preparing to leave Dallas, I grabbed some fast food for breakfast, filled my car with gas, and found a *shade tree* near a restaurant to spend some time with God. I prayed for him to give me peace, protection, praises to sing, patience, and, most of all, to show me the path to take to get out of the city. My original plan was to head east on Interstate 635, but traffic came to a halt a few miles ahead. Fortunately, I noticed that Interstate 35 was clear, so I promptly changed course and enjoyed a hassle-free drive through Dallas and Waco. I took a break in

Waco and answered texts from friends. I continued State Highway 6 to College Station with little traffic, all the while talking to God, thinking of cherished memories of my husband, and singing some hymns.

While approaching the city of Navasota, I noticed a large black cloud in the distance. I said to God, "Well, there seems to be one more storm for You to carry me through." And for sixteen miles, it was one of the worst thunderstorms I had ever driven through. I just kept telling God to take the steering wheel. There were accidents on the side of the road, heavy rain, low visibility, lots of water on the road, and emergency vehicles racing by me. When I finally got through the stormy area, there was no rain and a beautiful, bright, sunny sky. God did indeed take me through another storm. This time, the storm was a physical one surrounded by dangerous rain, thunder and lightning, and scary traffic on the two-lane highway. I just kept praising God for His protection.

Safely arriving home, I remembered my prayer *under the shade tree* that morning. I was so grateful to God, who so faithfully provided all my needs that day, proving to me again that he continues to keep me "sheltered" on the easy paths as well as through the storms of life. Yes, God gave me guidance, peace, patience, protection, and praises to sing to Him along the way.

YOUR THOUGHTS

✓ Tell about a situation in your life when you sensed you were in danger.
✓ Are there times when you knew you were being sheltered in the arms of God?

_____

_____

_____

_____

_____

_____

GOD'S WORD

❖ *But let all who take refuge in you be glad; let them ever sing for joy. Spread your protection of them so that those who love your name may rejoice in you. Surely, LORD, you bless the righteous; you surround them with your favor as with a shield.* Psalm 5:11-12

❖ *The Lord your God is with you, a Mighty Warrior who saves. He will take great delight in you; in his love he will no longer rebuke you but will rejoice over you with singing.* Zephaniah 3:17

❖ *My salvation and my honor depend on God; he is my rock and my refuge. Trust him at all times, you people; pour out your hearts to him, for God is our refuge.* Psalm 62:7-8

❖ *You have been a refuge for the poor, a refuge for the needy in their distress, a shelter from the storm and a shade in the heat.* Isaiah 25:4

HYMNS FOR TODAY

 Sheltered in the Arms of God (Dottie Rambo)

> *Lord Jesus, I thank You for loving us as Your Holy Bride.*

During the first few days in July 2021, my life was busy working with other women to plan a churchwide event for women of all ages (including our teenagers) at FBC Conroe. We prayed for God's presence as we worshiped Him and fellowship in His name and ministered to older ladies the next day, sharing our love and flowers with them.

My mind was flooded with thoughts and ideas as God spoke to me concerning my connecting with the ones that He put in my heart. I continued to depend on Him for all things. One morning, as I was preparing for my personal worship time with God, I played the song *The Church's One Foundation*. As I sang the phrase, "He came and sought His Holy Bride," my heart felt such a powerful love from the Father.

Yes, I know Jesus came to die for me, to save me for eternal life in heaven. I had already spent some time that morning weeping still over the loss of my husband, and then I pondered how, in our marriage, we had been one in Christ, part of his Holy Bride. Jesus' great love for us is like a groom's love for His bride, and He desires for us to join Him for eternity. Oh, how God wants to gather us all into His presence now and for eternity! Yes, Jesus will return one day to collect His church. We are so loved with an almost indescribable love.

I long for the day when my Spirit will be in glory with the Father, the Son, and my beloved husband. And oh, the joy of being with all the saints, especially family and those who touched my life here on earth, as we spend eternity in God's presence.

YOUR THOUGHTS

✓ What words do you have to describe a bride?

✓ Why do you think the church is called "His Holy Bride"?

_____

_____

_____

_____

_____

_____

_____

_____

_____

_____

GOD'S WORD

❖ *Husbands, love your wives, just as Christ loved the church and gave himself up for her to make her holy, cleansing her by the washing with water through the word, and to present her to himself as a radiant church without stain, or wrinkle, or any other blemish, but holy and blameless.* Ephesians 5:25-27

❖ *The Lord himself will come down from heaven, with a loud command with the voice of the archangel and with the trumpet call of God, and the dead in Christ will rise first. After that those of us who are still alive will be caught up together with them in the clouds to meet the Lord in the air. And so we will be with the Lord forever.* I Thessalonians 4:16-17

❖ *Then I heard what sounded like a great multitude, like the roaring of rushing waters and like loud peals of thunder, shouting: "Hallelujah! For the Lord God Almighty reigns! Let us rejoice and be glad and give him glory! For the wedding of the Lamb has come, and his bride has made herself ready. Fine linen, bright and clean, was given her to wear."* Revelation 19:7-8

HYMNS FOR TODAY

 Triumphantly the Church Will Rise (L. Kirk Talley)

> *God, I rejoice in Your Heavenly Sunlight that helps me to see You in the journeys of my life.*

As life moved on, I found myself in different places and situations. I traveled from Dallas to San Diego in July 2021 to visit family for two weeks. There, I was in crowded airports, socially distancing and wearing masks for five to six hours. Flying alone for the first time made me feel lonely and challenged at times. I did a lot of observing, questioning, and praying as I maneuvered through the airports.

My son-in-law had arranged for my tickets, and so in Dallas, I was in the first group to board with no assigned seats. I discovered a window seat next to a kind young man who promptly helped me place my backpack in the overhead storage. The plane was packed with people, and I was glad to be alone by a window as I was so emotional the entire trip.

When we finally landed in San Diego. I quickly found my way to baggage claim, where my daughter, with all hugs and smiles, greeted me. It was relaxing to enjoy a nice, quiet lunch in the old part of San Diego. We then traveled to Encinitas, where I would stay with my daughter, her husband, and my three grandchildren.

It was a wonderful time being with them. We spent time together at a mountain resort, walked on the beach, and just enjoyed being with each other. I also spent a couple of days with Max's sister and her husband in Riverside. I loved the cool, comfortable weather near the coast and would sometimes even sit out by their pool (under a big umbrella) while working on this writing. We celebrated birthdays, as well as mine and Max's anniversary. What a special treat it was to spend time one-on-one with my grandchildren!

One of my husband's favorite Bible teachers was Dr. David Jeremiah, so we made plans to attend his church in Encinitas on a Sunday. It was a small satellite church, and I was at first disappointed that Dr. Jeremiah was not preaching that day on the live stream. But oh, how blessed we were to hear another minister speak on Family

Foundations in Christ. While we were leaving the church, my daughter mentioned that the minister's remarks reminded her of her dad's actions and words.

On Wednesday, August 11, I returned to Dallas. The airport in San Diego was crowded, and the flight was packed. So again, I knew I had to trust God to take care of me, especially when finding my way around the airport in Dallas. The next day, I rested, and then on Friday, I drove to Cameron, Texas, where Max and I had lived for eight years early in our marriage.

My friends Linda and Maxie had invited me to spend the night with them. What a blessing it was to reminisce about such happy times in my life and to be with such loving longtime friends. While driving home on Saturday, I felt so refreshed as I had seemed to experience a renewal just being with family and friends. I did not realize how much I needed that time to continue in my grieving process.

During the span of three weeks, I covered numerous miles and observed God's love and care each day. I praise God for the Heavenly Sunlight that continues to carry me through my journeys and for the joys of being with my loved ones and friends. During my lifetime, I have been privileged to experience travels for pleasure as well as to serve my Lord, and in all of them, I have always seen God's guidance and blessings.

YOUR THOUGHTS

- ✓ Share the details of a memorable trip you've taken.
- ✓ How do you see God in your traveling experiences?

_____

_____

_____

_____

_____

_____

_____

_____

_____

_____

GOD'S WORD

❖ *Whoever dwells in the shelter of the Most High will rest in the shadow of the Almighty. I will say of the LORD, "He is my refuge and my fortress, my God, in whom I will trust."* Psalm 91:1-2

❖ *The LORD will keep you from all harm--he will watch over your life; the LORD will watch over your coming and going both now and forevermore.* Psalm 121:7-8

❖ *The Lord makes firm the steps of the one who delights in him; though he may stumble, he will not fall for the LORD holds him up with his hand.* Psalm 37:23-24

❖ *My son, do not let wisdom and understanding out of your sight, preserve sound judgment and discretion; they will be life to you, an ornament to grace your neck. Then you will go on your way in safety, and you will not stumble.* Proverbs 3:21-23

❖ *For God, who said, "Let light shine out of darkness," made his light to shine in our hearts to give us the light of the knowledge of God's glory displayed in the face of Christ.* 2 Corinthians 4:6

HYMNS FOR TODAY

 Heavenly Sunlight (Henry J. Zelley, 1899)

> *God, I rejoice and give thanks for Your*
> *cleansing power in my life.*

While sitting on my deck *under the shade tree* one beautiful morning, I pondered the happenings of life, which included the fact that COVID was still with us in variant forms. One thing that had changed for all of us was the importance of keeping ourselves protected from the virus. Lysol cleaners, hand wipes, and hand sanitizers were in our homes and our cars. We could try to handle that situation quickly, but I wondered if people were as concerned about their spiritual lives. I hoped people were calling on God to cleanse their spiritual lives, which is very important. In one of my husband's Bibles, I found an old note with these words:

"We do not need to be holier than thou, but we do need to be HOLY.
We don't need to be puritanical, but we do need to be PURE.
We don't need to be goody, goody, but we do need to be GOOD."

Those are words of wisdom and are essential for our daily living. My prayer is for all people to accept in faith the cleansing power of the blood of Jesus that purifies our hearts and minds, filling us with a desire to reverence and please God. Yes, that purification presents us to God as blameless and unstained with guilt. That cleansing gives us the Holy Spirit, empowering us to live holy and righteous lives as we share the goodness of God with others. It is in our humble obedience to God that we can truly enjoy living a clean and healthy spiritual life that will honor God as we are blessed with His joy and peace.

YOUR THOUGHTS

- ✓ How do you interpret being *holy, pure, and good*?
- ✓ How do we apply those things in our daily life?

_____

_____

_____

_____

_____

_____

_____

_____

_____

_____

GOD'S WORD

- ❖ *How much more, then, will the blood of Christ, who through the eternal Spirit offered himself unblemished to God, cleanse our consciences from acts that lead to death, so that we may serve the living God.* Hebrews 9:14

- ❖ *To the church of God in Corinth, to those sanctified in Christ Jesus and called to be his holy people, together with all those everywhere who call on the name of the Lord Jesus Christ--their Lord and ours: Grace and peace to you from God our Father and the Lord Jesus Christ.* I Corinthians 1:2-3

- ❖ *If we walk in the light, as he is in the light, we have fellowship with one another, and the blood of Jesus, his Son, purifies us from all sin.* I John 1:7

❖ *Finally brothers, whatever is true, whatever is noble, whatever is right, whatever is pure, whatever is lovely, whatever is admirable—if anything is excellent or praiseworthy—think about these things. Whatever you have learned or have received or heard from me and seen in me—put it into practice. And the God of peace will be with you.* Philippians 4:8-9

❖ *With this in mind, we constantly pray for you, that our God may make you worthy of his calling, and that by his power He may bring to fruition your every desire for goodness and every deed be prompted by faith.* 2 Thessalonians 1:11

HYMNS FOR TODAY

 Sanctuary, Lord Prepare Me (Randy Scruggs and John W. Thompson)

> *God, I am so grateful for Your Spirit as You carry on Your good works in our lives on earth.*

There's only one small magnet on the door of my stainless-steel refrigerator. My husband put it there a few years ago. It is a small wooden cross with the words *Carry On* and the scripture Philippians 1:6.

Early one September morning in 2021, as I entered the kitchen, that small cross seemed to stare at me. I have always known it was there, but that morning, it seemed to send me a message from Max that he wanted me to carry on. I immediately thought of how God must have had my husband put that cross there just for me at this time in my life. It was indeed an affirmation of my continuing to let God live in me as He would lead me.

Sometimes, life on this earth is challenging so that we might isolate ourselves from the will of the Father. It is easy to get caught up in our problems, fears, disagreements, and selfish desires. But as Christians, we must dedicate ourselves daily to being filled with His Spirit and, in faith, know that God will carry on His good work in us as we allow Him to.

Yes, my dear husband would want me to carry on with this life as God has planned. It was as if Max was telling me, "We were 'one' for fifty years on earth, and we are still 'one' in the Spirit. God began his good work in you [Gail] when you were nine years old when you trusted Jesus as your Savior. God is just keeping you on earth a while longer to be used in His Kingdom there, so CARRY ON!"

Through the power of the Holy Spirit, God has always done His work through us, and He will continue to do so in the spreading of His Word and His love. Let us CARRY ON!

YOUR THOUGHTS

✓ Has God used a loved one or the memory of someone to speak to you?
✓ What are some ways you see God "carrying on His good work" in His people?

_____

_____

_____

_____

_____

_____

_____

_____

_____

_____

GOD'S WORD

❖ *I thank God every time I remember you. In all my prayers for all of you, I always pray with joy because of your partnership in the gospel from the first day until now. I am being confident that God who began a good work in you will carry it on to completion until the day of Christ Jesus.* Philippians 1:3-6

❖ *Jesus said, "Very truly I tell you, whoever believes in me will also do the works I have been doing and they will do even greater works than these, because I am going to the Father."* John 14:12

❖ *Therefore, my friends, as you have always obeyed -- not only as in my presence, but much now much more in my absence – continue to work out your salvation with fear and trembling, for it is God who works through you, both to will and work for his good pleasure.* Philippians 2:12-13

❖ *Christ is the one we proclaim, admonishing, and teaching everyone with all wisdom so that we may present everyone fully mature in Christ. To this end I strenuously contend with all energy Christ so powerfully works in me.*
Colossians 1:28-29

HYMNS FOR TODAY

He Who Began a Good Work in You (Steve Green)
Until Then (Stuart Hamblen, 1958)

O God, on this Christmas Day, I rejoice in knowing that You have always known my heart and that Your Spirit has blessed me so richly.

As Christmas was approaching in 2021, there were some unusually warm days in Texas, so I found myself sitting on my deck *under the shade tree.* I was so missing my husband. But I knew he wanted me to "carry on" as God planned. Max had been an answer to my prayers. All during my youth, I prayed for God to one day give me a godly husband. During my college days, I had a poem by my bedside that was a prayer written by a young girl praying for the man God would one day give her. The poem, which had been cut from a magazine, did not have a name on it, so I never knew who wrote it. But it was so special to me, and I continued to dwell on it daily, trusting God. Through the years, I have shared that poem with teenagers.

Max and I met a year after college graduation while teaching in Killeen, Texas, and were married in August 1970. We had been married for fifty years when Max went to his heavenly home. So, this was my second Christmas without him. As I awoke on December 25, 2021, for the first time in my life, I was utterly alone in my house on a Christmas morning. It hit me hard, and I cried, remembering every Christmas with my husband over the past fifty years.

There was only one small gift under my Christmas tree. It is so different from many gifts that we have shared in the past. But why gifts? What gift had I cherished the most? What was the gift that God allowed me to use? And why should a gift be so significant? Many presents that we unwrap are long forgotten. We mostly give a gift because we love another. I think about the intangible gifts that are so much more cherished.

As I look back on my life, I see the many gifts that God gave me through my husband. The more I think about Max's life, the more I cherish his allowing the fruit of the Spirit to be evident in his life. Max loved me profoundly and loved his family unconditionally. He patiently walked by my side, prayed and worshiped with me, and provided the gentle support that I needed daily. He respected me as his wife, as well as my relationship with God. He talked and laughed with me and held my hand often as we traveled many miles together.

Max was always so willing for us to serve joyfully together in many ways as God led. He also gave me the gift of time to serve in ways that he knew God led me. My husband always showed his appreciation to me for the ways I loved him and served him as his wife. One of his most admired qualities was that Max was a humble man who never bragged about himself or talked about the things he had done. So, I cherish all the intangible gifts that God gave me through my husband, who loved and served God in his easygoing way of life. A life that never was rude or disrespectful to others. He was dedicated to loving God with all his heart, his soul, his mind, and his strength, as well as loving others. I mostly treasure the way Max had a strong relationship with God and spent so much time reading God's word. Those words became so real in his life, and in his quiet, loving way, Max shared them with others that God put in his path.

When Evangelist Billy Graham left this earth for his heavenly home in 2018, I watched the live broadcast of his funeral service at the Billy Graham Library in Charlotte, North Carolina; I enjoyed seeing one of his daughters read a poem that her mother had written when she was young. To my amazement, I immediately recognized it as being the prayer that I had read and prayed while I was in college. Ruth Graham, the wife of Billy Graham, had written my prayer! How touching it was to know that those words she had prayed for *her* Graham had been the same ones I had prayed for *my* Graham.

God is so faithful! One of the most significant memories for me is that on our fortieth wedding anniversary, Max and I traveled to North Carolina and toured the Billy Graham childhood home and library.

On Christmas night, when my son and I arrived home from spending the day with longtime friends (Morgan and Moore families) in College Station, I again noticed the one small gift under the tree that I had not opened. It was a pretty journal with these words on the front: "I know the plans I have made for you." The gift was from my daughter, who is growing in her faith and understanding the plans God has for her. We then Face-Timed Stephanie and her family in California and enjoyed our time together.

Greg's gift to me was "being here with me," as well as a large, framed print of his photograph of the snow-covered Rocky Mountain peaks with the beautiful fall foliage. As I enjoy looking at it daily, I am reminded of my awesome God and His creation and the memorable trips that Max and I enjoyed taking to the Rocky Mountains.

As I went to bed that night thinking about the sad and the happy moments of that Christmas Day, my thoughts turned again to how I had been so blessed to have had Max in my life. I know Max could not have lived the life he did without a loving *Savior*. We would not have had the blessed marriage that we had enjoyed without our *Savior*. I am so grateful that my greatest gift is Jesus, who is our joyous gift of salvation, our abundant life here on earth, and a hope of eternal life with Him. Great is thy faithfulness to me, O, Lord!

YOUR THOUGHTS

✓ How has accepting Jesus Christ as your Savior impacted your life?
✓ Why must the fruit of the Holy Spirit be evident in the lives of believers?

_____

_____

_____

_____

_____

_____

_____

_____

_____

_____

GOD'S WORD

❖ *Today in the town of David, a Savior has been born to you; he is the Messiah, the Lord.* Luke 2:11

❖ *Salvation is found in no one else, for there is no other name under heaven given to mankind by which we must be saved.* Acts 4:12

❖ *The fruit of the Spirit is love, joy, peace, patience, kindness, goodness, faithfulness, gentleness, and self-control. Against such things there is no law* Galatians 5:22-23

❖ *"For I know the plans I have for you," declares the LORD, "plans to prosper you and not to harm you, plans to give you hope and a future."* Jeremiah 29:11

❖ *Each of you should use whatever gift you have received to serve others, as faithful stewards of God's grace in its various forms. If anyone speaks, they should do so as one who speaks the very words of God. If anyone serves, they should do so with the strength that God provides so that in all things God may be praised through Jesus Christ. To him be the glory and the power forever and forever!* I Peter 4:10-11

HYMNS FOR TODAY

O, What a Savior (Marvin P. Dalton, 1948)
Great is Thy Faithfulness (Thomas O. Chisholm, 1923)

> *Dear God, I want to be filled with Your Spirit and to worship and serve You continuously.*

As my life continued in a new year, I did Bible studies with women in our church. It was wonderful to listen to God in planning and leading these studies for ten years. Yes, the best part is women meeting together to pray and to study God's Word. Yet, also important is the blessing of sharing our faith with other women.

There had been so many new church members over the past year that over half of the women in our Monday morning study were new to our group. It was indeed a blessing to get to know them and to see God in their lives. When I am with a group of ladies who openly share their testimonies of God's faithfulness in their lives and sense the Holy Spirit leading us, I know we are in the presence of God. And then I receive texts and emails thanking me for allowing the Holy Spirit to lead. What a sweet, sweet spirit is in this group!

Serving in a leadership role for the women's ministry in our church was a great blessing. We appreciated so many new women serving in all aspects of our activities: Fall Market as a fundraiser for scholarships, a Christmas brunch, luncheons, dinners for scholarship recipients, and local missions. These are all enjoyable activities with a focus on our spiritual life. Still, to me, the real honor is to see women getting to know one another and building relationships that share God's love and His plan of salvation. God also provided for our FBC Literacy First to serve our community with ESL classes again, and what a blessing! Not only do we teach English, but we also learn and discuss Bible scriptures.

Yes, people observe my being busy in these activities, but there is so much more that gives me joy in serving my Lord and Savior. Only God sees the peace in my life when I take time to pray with women in their time of need. I am so blessed to text prayers and scriptures weekly with women who are hurting with significant issues in their lives. What a blessing to get to know new friends while at a local restaurant as we talk, laugh, and encourage one another.

Only God sees my ESL students come to me for prayer and support. What a blessing they are to me as I see their courage to live in a new country, learn a new language, and trust God for all their needs. And oh, how happy I am to get to know some of the younger women of our church and encourage them, especially in praying for them. And they do not realize what their big smiles and hugs do for me.

While enjoying my time *under the shade tree* in my backyard, I often think about who I am and where I am because I feel as though I have lost part of my identity. Then, the power of the Holy Spirit helps me to see that my life is not so much about my identity but about *my God and who He is in me*. The honesty of it all is that the more I serve my faithful God, the more I know Him and trust in Him, even as Satan is throwing darts at me all the while. Darts of insecurities and obstacles trying to keep me from obeying my Lord. When experiencing all the little issues that come up, I know that I must have the patience and wisdom to trust God to take care of them. Understanding that we deal with personality conflicts and selfish desires on this earth, I know that I must allow God to love others through me. I must humbly allow the *joy of the Lord to be my strength* in all He wants to "be" and "do" in me as I "carry on" in this life. Rejoicing daily in His presence is my deepest desire!

YOUR THOUGHTS

✓ How has praying and studying God's word with other Christians blessed you?
✓ How do you see God's presence in your life?

_____

_____

_____

_____

_____

_____

_____

_____

_____

_____

GOD'S WORD

❖ *As the deer pants for streams of water, so my soul pants for you, my God.*
Psalm 42:1

❖ *Let us consider how we may spur one another on toward love and good deeds, not giving up meeting together, as some are in the habit of doing, but encouraging one another—and all the more as you see the Day approaching.*
Hebrews 10:24-25

❖ *In your relationships with one another have the same mindset as Christ Jesus: Who, being the very nature of God, did not consider equality with God something to be used to his advantage. Rather he made himself nothing by taking the very nature of a servant, being made in human likeness. And being found in appearance as a man, he humbled himself by becoming obedient to death—even death on a cross!* Philippians 2:5-8

❖ *What we have received is not the spirit of the world, but the Spirit who is from God, so that we may understand what God has freely given us. This is what we speak, not in words taught by human wisdom but in words taught by the Spirit explaining spiritual realities with Spirit-taught words.* I Corinthians 2:12-13

❖ *For we are God's handiwork, created in Christ Jesus to do good works which God prepared in advance for us to do.* Ephesians 2:10

❖ *As for you, the anointing you received from God remains in you, and you do not need anyone else to teach you. But as his anointing teaches you about all things and as that anointing is real, not counterfeit—just as it taught you, remain in him.* I John 2:27

HYMNS FOR TODAY

As the Deer Pants for the Water (Martin J. Nystrom, 1981)
The Greatest Thing in All My Life (Mark D. Pendergrass, 1977)

> *Dear God, this world has troubles, and life is hard for many people. I pray that we humbly allow Your love to flow through us.*

As life goes on, I am content and blessed with my relationship with my Lord. However, I observe so much pain and suffering as people endure physical and mental illnesses and grieve losses of life. I see the hurt in families who have marital problems, rebellious youth, and many others with broken relationships. Many people in our communities struggle with financial needs. My heart aches as I observe the lonely, homeless men and women who come to our church for a hot meal.

Even as I enjoy my Christian fellowship with other believers, I look at our surroundings and see so many empty souls without a relationship with God. Many homes do not know or teach about Jesus to their children and youth. Selfish desires consume many people because Satan has deceived them about the truths of our Holy God. I pray that we, as Christians, can open their eyes by sharing the love of Jesus.

My daily prayer is for God to help us as believers follow His commands to love and minister to the needs of our hurting world. We remember that it is not our place to judge others. My prayer is that Christians become so burdened that we allow the Holy Spirit to lead us, speak through us, and genuinely share God's love with others. We must all be honest about our daily need for God in the realities of this life. I pray that as we look back at our past, we acknowledge His faithfulness to us. Let us be mindful that we are not so different from those who need us to share Jesus with them in our communities.

Our world has failed to be what God first created it to be. Yet, God is still loving and caring for all His creation, especially people. I see hurting people everywhere, including in my church congregation. Yes, God wants us to love and encourage each other through the Holy Spirit. I praise Him for leading us in our steps as we go through our days. Let us be open to the opportunities to minister to someone in the name of Jesus. Often, God has a person in our path to encourage us in our faith. We have learned that our faith grows and becomes more robust the more we share it with others. To God be the glory that in this fallen world, He is still supreme and victorious over Satan.

YOUR THOUGHTS

✓ How do you see our world today? Is it different from Biblical times?
✓ How do you see God using you in the lives of others who need to know Him?
✓ How do we share our faith?

_____

_____

_____

_____

_____

_____

_____

_____

_____

_____

GOD'S WORD

❖ *Jesus went through all the towns and villages teaching in their synagogues, proclaiming the good news of the kingdom and healing every disease and sickness. When He saw the crowds, Jesus had compassion on them because they* were harassed and helpless, like sheep without a shepherd. The He said to his disciples, "The harvest is plentiful, but the workers are few. Ask the Lord of the harvest to send workers into his harvest field." Matthew 9:35-37

❖ *For the Spirit God gave us does not make us timid, but gives us power, love, and self-discipline.* 2 Timothy 1:7

❖ *Be wise in the way you act toward outsiders; make the most of every opportunity.* Colossians 4:5

❖ *I pray that you may be active in sharing your faith, so that you will have a full understanding of every good thing we have in Christ.* Philemon 1:6

❖ *But in your hearts revere Christ as Lord. Always be prepared to give an answer to everyone who asks you to give the reason for the hope that you have. But do this with gentleness and respect.* I Peter 3:15-16

❖ *You, my dear children, are from God and have overcome them because the one who is in you is greater than the one who is in this world.* I John 4:4

HYMNS FOR TODAY

I Speak Jesus (Dustin Smith)
Redeemed, How I Love to Proclaim It (Fanny Crosby,1882)

O, the joy and peace of being in the Presence my Holy God!

I have spent many, many hours, days, and months seeking God in scriptures, praying, and singing hymns while writing and editing. Often, I spent time sitting *under a shade tree* and other times in the quietness of my home. What a blessing to be so absorbed in listening to God! In the hours of being in the presence of God, I am always so refreshed and filled with His peace and comfort.

One day, following several hours with God, I wrote these words about living in His presence.

Remembering all my days of real-life struggles,
I am never at peace unless I know my awesome God is with me.
In the busy days of life, I am never satisfied
unless I start my day in worship in the Holiness of God.
In all my relationships, I must sense
God is always living and loving through me.
In my serving, I thank God for being in me as He does His will.
In all my days, my God is with me,
filling me with so much love and joy.
In all my life, I am grateful for the power of the Holy Spirit in my life,
giving me the boldness to be a witness of my Lord.

What a blessing to participate in worship times with other Christians who honor our Lord and uplift us spiritually. But I am most grateful for the reverence and seeking of God during my daily times of worship as I honor Him and listen to Him. Yes, I genuinely know the presence of God in my sanctuary while praising His name.

Nothing compares with the presence of God in my life. To God be glory! I continuously sing: Hallelujah! He is holy, holy! Bless His name!

YOUR THOUGHTS

✓ How do you experience the holiness of God in your life?
✓ What is our Holy God doing in your life today?

_____

_____

_____

_____

_____

_____

_____

_____

_____

_____

GOD'S WORD

❖ *Worship the LORD in the splendor of his holiness; tremble before him, all the earth.* Psalm 96:9

❖ *And the Spirit of him who raised Jesus from the dead is living in you, he who raised Christ from the dead will also give life to your mortal bodies because of His Spirit who lives in you.* Romans 8:11

❖ *May the God of hope fill you with all joy and peace as you trust in him, so that you may overflow with hope by the power of the Holy Spirit.* Romans 15:13

❖ *May the Lord make your love increase and overflow for each other and for everyone else, just as our love does for you. May he strengthen your hearts so that you will be blameless and holy in the presence of our God and Father when Jesus comes with all his holy ones.* 1 Thessalonians 3:12-13

HYMNS FOR TODAY

He is Here (Kirk Talley)
Holy Ground (Geron Davis)

> *Dear God, I come humbly with a heart of praise for You as a Holy Sovereign God who is my Creator, my Salvation, a mighty Spirit living in me, my Sustainer of life, and my hope of eternal life with You.*

I am writing my closing words but acknowledging that God's presence in my life remains ongoing. Foremost, I am sure that our loving God seeks companionship with every individual, which is why I consistently offer praise and engage in worship and fellowship.

As Christians, we primarily communicate with each other about what God does in our lives through verbal communication. So, let us tell others about God's faithfulness in our lives. Life on earth can fill us with pain, sorrow, rejection, selfishness, and many other distractions that hinder us from truly experiencing a loving God. We worship a living God who is able and wants to help us in this life.

So, I pray that we all can be honest about our need for Him and our need to share Him with others. May we all realize that voicing a few words of praise to God can open the door to giving someone the opportunity to accept Jesus as Savior, to know the abundant life as a Christian, and to hope in heaven.

Everyone must have a relationship with God the Father through repentance of a sinful nature by accepting the blood sacrifice of Jesus, the Son. Then we can live daily in joy and peace through the leadership of the Holy Spirit. Life on earth is difficult, but with God at the center of all we do, life is much better as our faith grows and we learn to trust Him and serve Him more each day. Spending time daily meditating on God's Word and prayer is the key to knowing His peace in this chaotic world. Living in His Spirit, we learn to love as he loves, and we see His plans as we humbly surrender to Him.

God continues to give me times of affirmation of His promise of a heavenly home. Many days when I listen to music, the songs are about heaven. One morning in March 2022, as I was serving as a greeter at the door of our church, an older gentleman with weak knees struggled as he made his way up the steps. With a big smile on his face, he said, "I am so happy to be here, but I will be much happier when I get to heaven," as he pointed upward.

As I sat *under my shade tree* later that afternoon, I thought about my greeting time that morning. I realized I had been serving at the same door where my husband had stood two years before in March, greeting people with a smile while using his hand sanitizer. That day had been Max's last time in our church, where he had always enjoyed serving as a greeter.

Thinking about that gentleman's words really spoke to me. I again thought of the happiness that Max and I had experienced in our life together on earth and that we had shared so much joy in our place of worship on Sundays. Yet, what a blessing to think of *how much happier* Max is in his eternal place of rest with Jesus. Remembering that encounter, I rejoiced with weeping and praising God! Oh, the little things that God does to remind us of who He is and how He plans our lives to give us opportunities to see Him, to know Him, and to one day spend eternity with Him.

Appreciate the *shade trees* or any peaceful spaces that God offers for finding solitude in worship. Sometimes, our best worship is time spent with God *under a shade tree* as we seek and honor Him. It is in those solitary sanctuary times that He often fills our hearts with renewed peace and opens our eyes to see new visions of who He is in our lives.

HYMNS FOR TODAY

To God Be the Glory (Fanny Crosby,1875)
What a Day That Will Be (Jim Hill)

About the Author

Gail Graham grew up in Plano, Texas, along with her parents and four siblings. She graduated from East Texas Baptist University and enjoyed being an elementary teacher in public and private schools for thirty years. She and her husband, Max, were happily married for fifty years when Max went to his heavenly home in 2020. They loved family time with their two children and three grandchildren. Their favorite travels were to the Rocky Mountains. Their experience in public schools and church ministries throughout Texas always involved working with youth, which they enjoyed.

For the past twelve years, Gail has had the privilege of writing curriculum and teaching English Second Language classes in the Literacy First Ministry at FBC Conroe. Along with a few others, she formed *The English Club,* giving women from other countries the opportunity for conversation and building relationships while adjusting to life in Texas.

She teaches the Bible to women and children on Sunday mornings and sings in her church choir. She also helps plan and lead ladies' Bible studies and other church ministries for women that serve the needs of women in the church and the community.

Gail says, "The greatest joy in my life is to know Jesus as my Savior and to serve my God with the realization that God in the power of the Holy Spirit is living and loving through me. I desire for others to know God's love, joy, and peace as they experience God's faithfulness in the realities of life."

Contact Information

To contact the author regarding speaking engagements or bulk orders, visit: www.bgailgraham.com
or email: gmgram@aol.com.

Use for Group Study

Throughout my lifetime, God has always blessed my times with Him, but I received a special blessing while listening to Him in the writing of these words my Lord gave me. It is clear to me now that as I sat *under the shade trees,* God used that time for His purpose. I pray that God be glorified as readers spend time in Bible study and worship as they see God in their own lives.

Under the Shade Tree can be used as a group study. The purpose of a group study is to see and experience the faithfulness of God within our real-life situations in a worship setting as participants focus on scriptures and hymns while sharing their own experiences. The book is divided into nine sections, with a focus on one section at a time. Each person uses the book as they choose, with no requirement of homework.

PREPARATIONS FOR A GROUP STUDY

- The study can be completed over nine weeks, with 90 minutes or two-hour sessions at each meeting.
- A copy of *Under the Shade Tree* should be made available for each participant.
- A room with tables (preferably round) that seat four to six people at a table for small group time. The tables should be in one larger room to ensure privacy for the small group sessions, but participation in the full sessions.
- Media equipment should be made available for the presentation of downloaded music videos with lyrics. A microphone may be necessary if the meeting is held in a large area.

- A schedule of the nine weeks should be given to participants at the first session. This will list the dates, times, and title of the section of the book for each date.

PARTICIPATION IN THE WEEKLY SESSIONS

A large group leader will plan the agenda for the session and distribute copies to small group leaders. The agenda will include the pages to be discussed as well as the music to be used with the times listed for small group participation and large group participation. The large group leader will open and close each session, play the music videos, and keep the agenda flowing according to the schedule.

A small group leader for each table will keep the session going according to the time frame, with the reading and discussion of scriptures and questions listed on the agenda. It is helpful for the large group leader to meet with the small group leaders prior to each session to discuss the agenda for each day and have a prayer time. Keep in mind that all pages in the book will not be discussed in these sessions.

Access to media equipment for playing downloaded music videos with lyrics is vital to the worship time of this study. The media pastor can display videos on a large screen, making it convenient to play them when needed based on the day's schedule. There is no need for a music leader. Everyone joins in singing, preferably standing. A list of YouTube videos is included at the end of this chapter. Leaders may also select their own music through other sites.

The agenda for each day is based on the pages to be discussed and the hymns. The reading of scripture and the discussing of the questions is followed by a hymn that applies to that topic.

The following page contains a sample agenda for a session:

Before the Introduction, begin playing a hymn to show that the session is beginning and allow participants to redirect their attention and focus.

- Introduction and Prayer—5 minutes
- Small Group Time (held at the individual tables)—15 minutes
- Hymn Sing with the Entire Group—5 minutes
- Small Group Time—20 minutes
- Large Group Hymn Sing—5 minutes
- Small Group Time—15 minutes
- Large Group Hymn Sing—5 minutes
- Small Group Time—15 minutes
- Closing Hymn and Prayer

These suggestions are for a large group setting, but some people enjoy having a small group study in their homes. Please consider using *Under the Shade Tree* with your small group setting, which will give you the opportunity to enjoy sharing scriptures, discussing the questions, and singing the hymns. Jesus says He is "in our midst" no matter the size of the group.

PURPOSE OF A GROUP STUDY

Through group studies, people can share their personal experiences of God while reading His Word and worshiping together. The small group time encourages people to participate in short discussions of the topics and questions of each session. By reading and discussing the scriptures, participants can better understand how those words apply to their lives. The act of singing hymns together creates a powerful atmosphere of communal worship in reverence to God. Yet, each song can give a powerful message to individuals as they participate.

Whether used in a large group, small group, or even women's retreat, I believe that *Under the Shade Tree* will be a blessing. Remember, it is not so much about our lives but all about experiencing God in the reality of our lives.

LIST OF HYMNS ON YOUTUBE

Using music videos of hymns enhances the study of scripture and worship while reading and discussing the book *Under the Shade Tree*. Listed are some YouTube suggestions that have been used for each section of the book. The list includes the length of each video. Readers have the option to find their own music videos.

KNOWING GOD IN UNEXPECTED CHALLENGES

- *A Mighty Fortress is Our God*
  (lyrics) by Michael W. Smith Praise Adonai YouTube July 16, 2016
  3:51

- *Immortal, Invisible, God Only Wise - Great Are You Lord*
  (lyrics)w orship4christ 2012 YouTube 5/5/2013   3:46

- *Hear Our Prayer O Lord*
  (No lyrics) YouTube Cynthia Clawson/Prayer and Plainsong 2010   1:31

- *Sweet Hour of Prayer*
  (lyrics) Don Marsh Orchestra Extended Life Worship YouTube 11/26/2020
                                                          2:58

- *You Raise Me Up*
  (lyrics) Josh Groban YouTube, toomuchfun09 6/10/2012   5:00

- *Lord, Be Glorified*
  (lyrics) The Maranatha Singers YouTube Extended Life Worship 3/26/2016
  3:06

SEEKING GOD IN DAILY STRUGGLES

- *Step by Step, O God You Are My God* by Rich Mullins
  (lyrics) YouTube Islington Baptist Church   3/12/2014   2:08

- *Shine, Jesus, Shine*
  (lyrics)   Maranatha! Music YouTube 6/15/2016   2:26

- *All Creatures of Our God and King*
  (lyrics)   YouTube md1801   2/21/2013   3:57

- *All That Thrills My Soul is Jesus*
  (lyrics)   YouTube Islington Baptist Church 1/10/2011   2:58

- *People Need the Lord*
  (lyrics) George Adaclog   YouTube   6/14/2009   4:41

- *All to Jesus I Surender*
  (lyrics) Worship Video   YouTube 7/31/2007   3:42

EXPERIENCING GOD IN SPIRITUAL HEALING

- *I'd Rather Have Jesus*
  (lyrics)   Islington Baptist Church YouTube 3/18/2010   4:21

- *The Church Triumphant*
  (lyrics) Manna International Ministry YouTube 1/16/2021   6:47

- *Blessed Assurance*
  (lyrics)   Northern Baptist Assoc. YouTube 6/25/2009   3:41

- *Thy Word*
  (lyrics) Amy Grant Mi Amor Channel YouTube 3/28/2013   3:20

- *The Blood Will Never Lose Its Power*
  (lyrics) Extended Life Worship YouTube 3/12/2017   4:16

- *We Are the Body of Christ*
  (lyrics) Leora Fleming   YouTube 8/1/2016   4:37

- *Have Faith in God When Your Pathway is Lonely*
  (lyrics) YouTube Squirrel 24   4/4/2021   2:50

SEEING GOD IN RESTING, REFLECTING, AND TRUSTING

- *Near to the Heart of God*
  (lyrics) YouTube SE Samonte 11/25/2013   3:27

- *God Give Us Christian Homes*
  (lyrics) Melharmonic Music Services Virtual Choir 2/24/2022   4:44

- *In His Presence*
  (lyrics) Sandi Patty YouTube The Christian OPM   2/6/2012   4:50

- *God Will Take Care of You*
  (lyrics) Cheer Up Music   Heritage Singers YouTube 6/1/2023   3:27

- *Do They See Jesus in Me*
  (lyrics) The Clark Family Cin music lyrics YouTube 5/4/2021   4:11

- *The Lord's My Shepherd*
  (lyrics)   Stuart Townend   Trinity Fellowship YouTube 11/2//2012   4:04

HONORING GOD IN PRAISING, SHARING, CELEBRATING, AND LISTENING

- *Let's Just Praise the Lord*
  (lyrics) Songs 4 Worship Extended Life Worship YouTube 1/15/2017   1:34

- *Wonderful Grace of Jesus*
  (lyrics) Islington Baptist Church   YouTube 7/28/2010   2:34

- *I Will Share His Love*
  (lyrics) Sung by Nancy Price YouTube Don Besig 5/2/2021   3:14

- *He Has Been So Faithful to Me*
  (lyrics)   The Brooklyn Tabernacle Choir, with testimony by Carol Cymbala, Sung by TaRanda Greene   YouTube 9/20/2019   10:40

BEING ANCHORED IN GOD'S LOVE, GRACE, PEACE, AND HOPE

- *It is Well with My Soul*
  (lyrics) Hymn Sing Along Staccy Plays Hymns, YouTube 1/29/2023   4:31

- *The Servant Song*
  (lyrics) servant of the lion YouTube 2/26/2010   3:05

- *The Anchor Holds*
  (lyrics) Ray Bolz   van lady 21 YouTube 1/19/2010   5:55

- *How Deep the Father's Love*

(lyrics) Stuart Towned ExaltHIMvdo YouTube 4/8/2022   3:31

- *Hymn of Praise*
  (lyrics) Gaither Vocal Band Easy Worship Resources, YouTube 8/17/2012
  3:50

- *Peace, Wonderful Peace*
  (lyrics) Heritage Singers   Perlynette YouTube 5/9/2018   2:19

BEING THANKFUL FOR GOD'S PEACE, PROMISES, PRESENCE, AND GOODNESS

- *Everlasting God*
  (lyrics) Maranatha Music YouTube Maranatha! Music 3/20/2015   4:19

- *Standing on the Promises*
  (lyrics) Christian Gospel Choir YouTube Worship Videos 1/1/2016   2:30

- *My Tribute*
  (lyrics) BTS Ministry YouTube 7/8/2020   3:35

- *Give Thanks*
  (lyrics) Richard Yap   YouTube 1/2/2012   3:34

- *Goodness of God*
  (lyrics) Bethel Music   music meets heaven YouTube 2/8/2019   5:04

- *God is So Good*
  (lyrics) Yancy Infinity Point One YouTube 9/6/2014   2:20

- *I Then Shall Live*
  (lyrics) The Gaither Vocal Band   justinnichols5 YouTube 11/5/2009 5:53
     Or
  (lyrics) Parkwood SDA Church YouTube   5/20/2023   5:33

PRAISING GOD FOR HIS LOVE, GUIDANCE, PROVISION, AND COMFORT

- *Stand Up, Stand Up for Jesus*
  (lyrics) UMH514 YouTube HaytiUMC   9/30/2015   2:57

- *All the Way My Savior Leads Me*
  (lyrics) Northern Lights Hymns The Haven Quartet YouTube 2/15/2012 2:45

- *My Faith Looks Up to Thee*
  (lyrics) Islington Baptist Church YouTube 3/23/2010   2:50

- *He Will Hold Me Fast*
  (lyrics) Selah   Jorge Velez   YouTube 5/28.2022   5:04

- *Precious Memories*
  (lyrics) Slim Whitman Easy Worship Resources YouTube 9/15/2015   3:37

- *Be Still My Soul*
  (lyrics) Celtic Thunder   YouTube Dalila Perez   11/10/2017   3:19

REJOICING IN LIFE

- *The Greatest Thing in All My Life*
  (lyrics) Mark Pendergrass HD 1080p Worship Songs YouTube 9/12/2015
     3:35

- *Sheltered in the Arms of God*
  (lyrics) West Creek Harmony YouTube 4/15/2013   2:43

- *Heavenly Sunlight*
  (lyrics) The Gaithers onyxshepherd08 YouTube 9/6/2018   2:42

- *Until Then*
  (lyrics) The Haven Quartet Easy Worship Resources YouTube 6/27/2015
  4:13

- *As the Deer*
  (lyrics) Maranatha! Singers Worship Video YouTube 6/3/2007   3:05

- *He Is Here*
  (lyrics) Gaither Vocal Band Extended Life Worship YouTube 9/13/2019
                                                                  6:34

- *He Is Here*
  (lyrics) Grace Larson Brumley The Anointing Makes the Difference YouTube
  7/2/2022   4:06

- *To God Be the Glory*
  (lyrics) Northern Baptist Association YouTube 11/30/2008   3:10

Made in the USA
Columbia, SC
28 February 2025

54265950R00157